GRAPHIC BIOGRAPHIES

BOOKER T. WASHINGTON
Great American Educator

by Eric Braun

illustrated by Cynthia Martin

Consultant:

Dr. Kenneth Goings, Professor and Chair

Department of African American and African Studies

Ohio State University, Columbus, Ohio

Capstone press

Mankato, Minnesota

Graphic Library is published by Capstone Press,
1710 Roe Crest Drive, North Mankato, Minnesota 56003.
www.capstonepub.com

Printed in the United States of America in Stevens Point, Wisconsin.
122011 006527WZVMI

Library of Congress Cataloging-in-Publication Data
Braun, Eric.
Booker T. Washington: great American educator / by Eric Braun; illustrated by Cynthia Martin.
p. cm.—(Graphic library. Graphic biographies)
Includes bibliographic references and index.
ISBN-13: 978-0-7368-4630-1 (hardcover) ISBN-10: 0-7368-4630-1 (hardcover)
ISBN-13: 978-0-7368-6190-8 (softcover pbk.) ISBN-10: 0-7368-6190-4 (softcover pbk.)
1. Washington, Booker T., 1856–1915—Juvenile literature. 2. African Americans—Biography—Juvenile literature. 3. Educators—United States—Biography—Juvenile literature. I. Martin, Cynthia, 1961– ill. II. Title. III. Series.
E185.97.W4B73 2006
370'.92—dc22 2005001727

Summary: In graphic novel format, tells the life story of Booker T. Washington and his accomplishments toward promoting the education of African Americans.

Art Direction
Jason Knudson

Designer
Jason Knudson

Editor
Blake A. Hoena

Editor's note: Direct quotations from primary sources are indicated by a yellow background.

Direct quotations appear on the following pages:

Pages 15, 18, 19, from *Up from Slavery: An Autobiography* by Booker T. Washington (West Berlin, N.J.: Townsend Press, 2004).

Page 22, from *Booker T. Washington: Great Lives Observed*, edited by Emma Lou Thornbrough (Englewood Cliffs, N.J.: Prentice-Hall, 1969).

Page 24, from *The Promise of the New South: Life after Reconstruction* by Edward L. Ayers (New York: Oxford University Press, 1992).

TABLE OF CONTENTS

Chapter 1

Slavery and Freedom

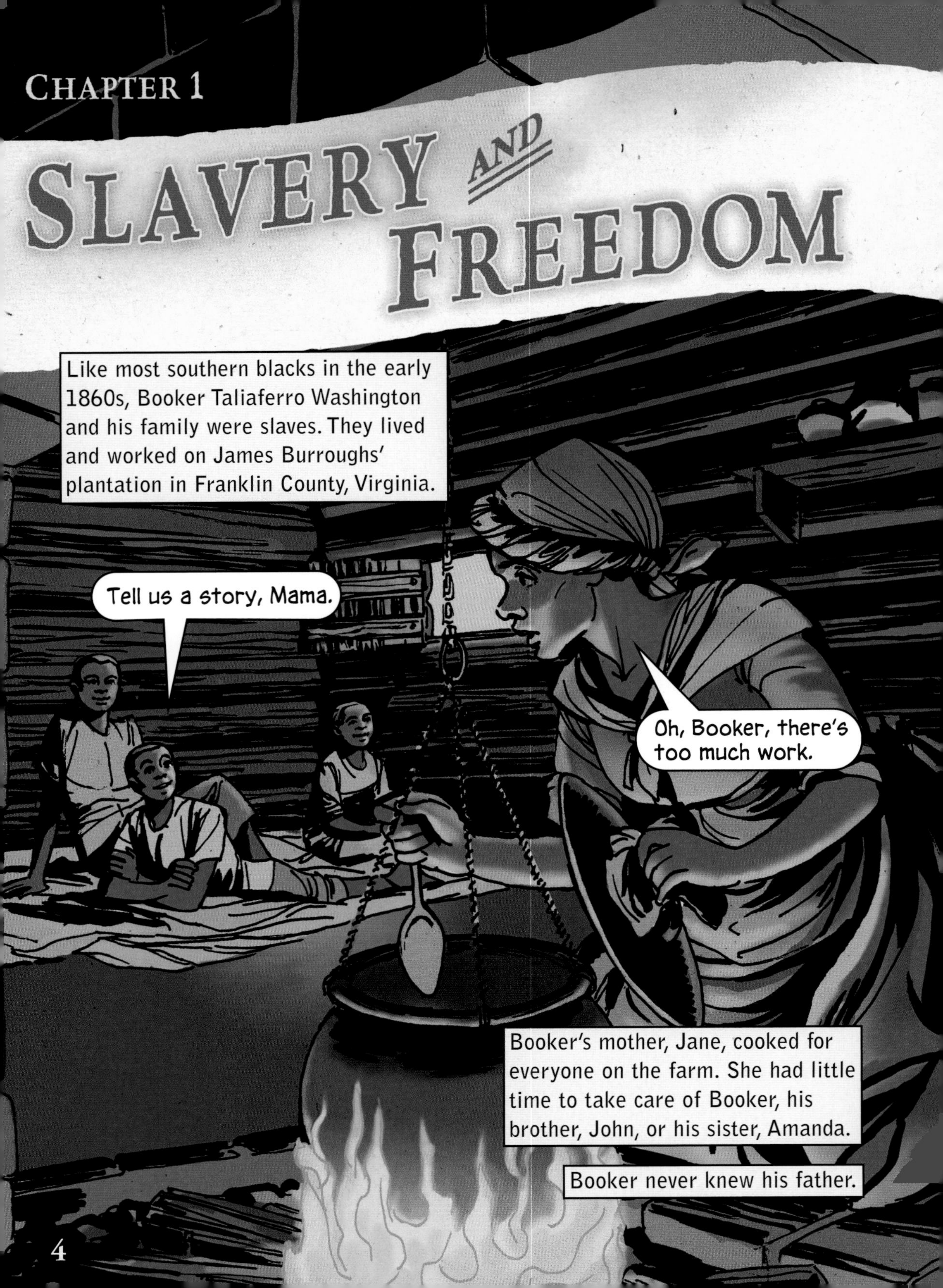

Like most southern blacks in the early 1860s, Booker Taliaferro Washington and his family were slaves. They lived and worked on James Burroughs' plantation in Franklin County, Virginia.
Tell us a story, Mama.
Oh, Booker, there's too much work.
Booker's mother, Jane, cooked for everyone on the farm. She had little time to take care of Booker, his brother, John, or his sister, Amanda.
Booker never knew his father.

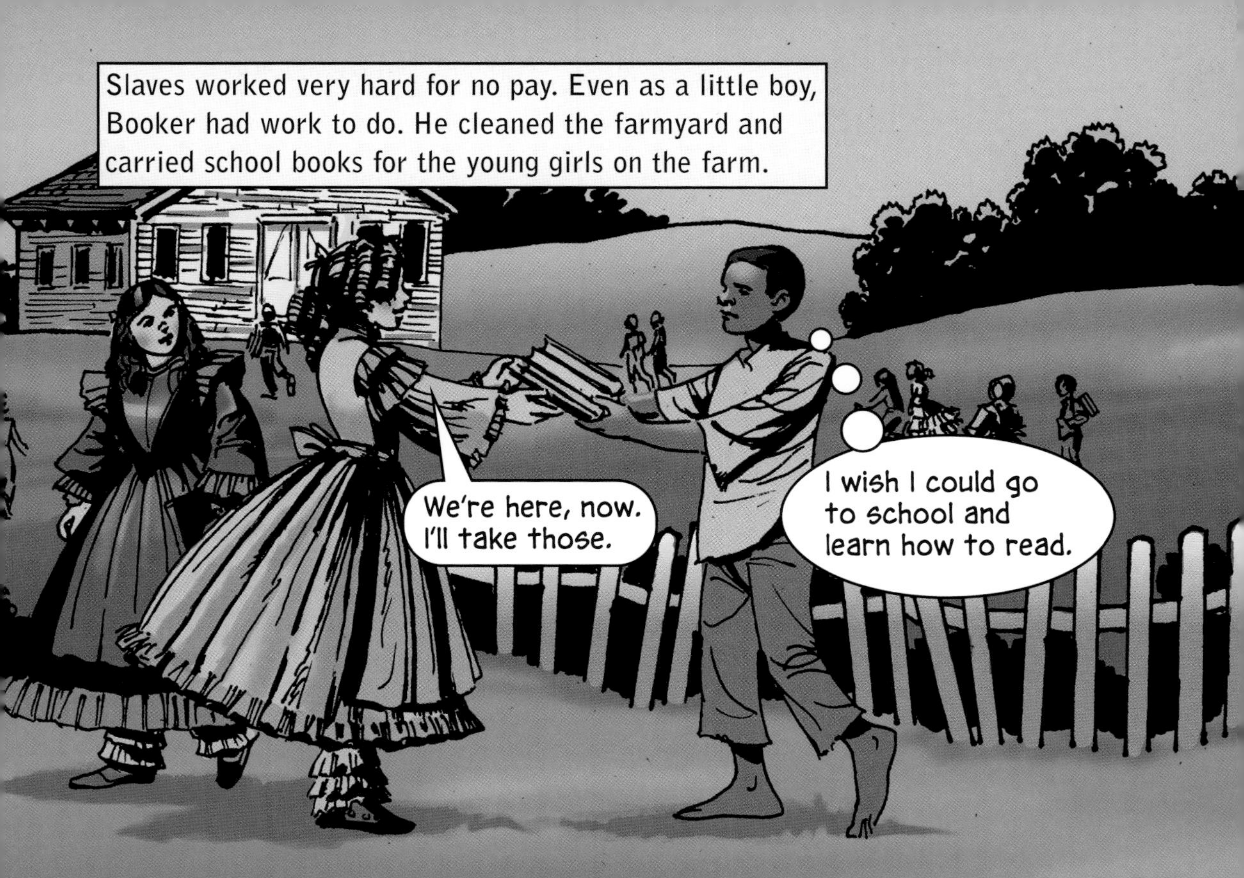
Slaves worked very hard for no pay. Even as a little boy, Booker had work to do. He cleaned the farmyard and carried school books for the young girls on the farm.
We're here, now. I'll take those.
I wish I could go to school and learn how to read.

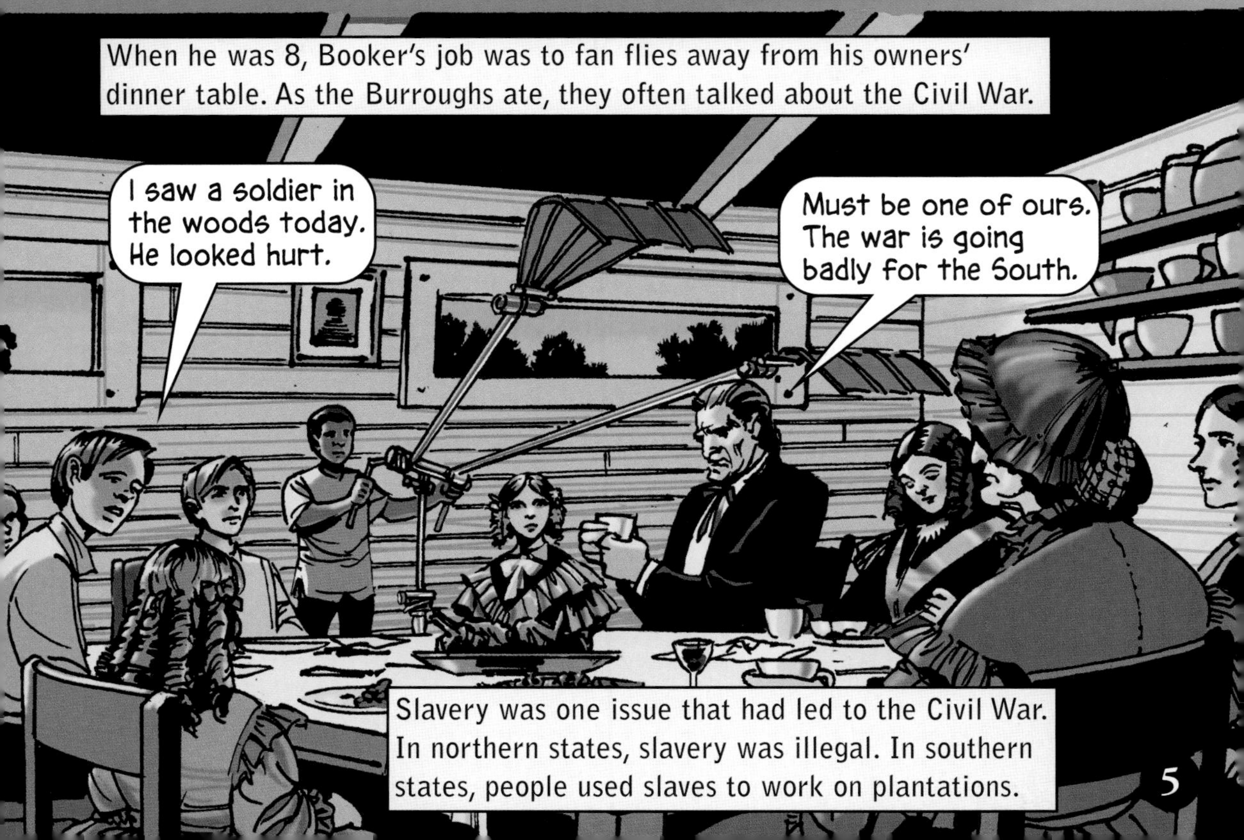
When he was 8, Booker's job was to fan flies away from his owners' dinner table. As the Burroughs ate, they often talked about the Civil War.
I saw a soldier in the woods today. He looked hurt.
Must be one of ours. The war is going badly for the South.
Slavery was one issue that had led to the Civil War. In northern states, slavery was illegal. In southern states, people used slaves to work on plantations.

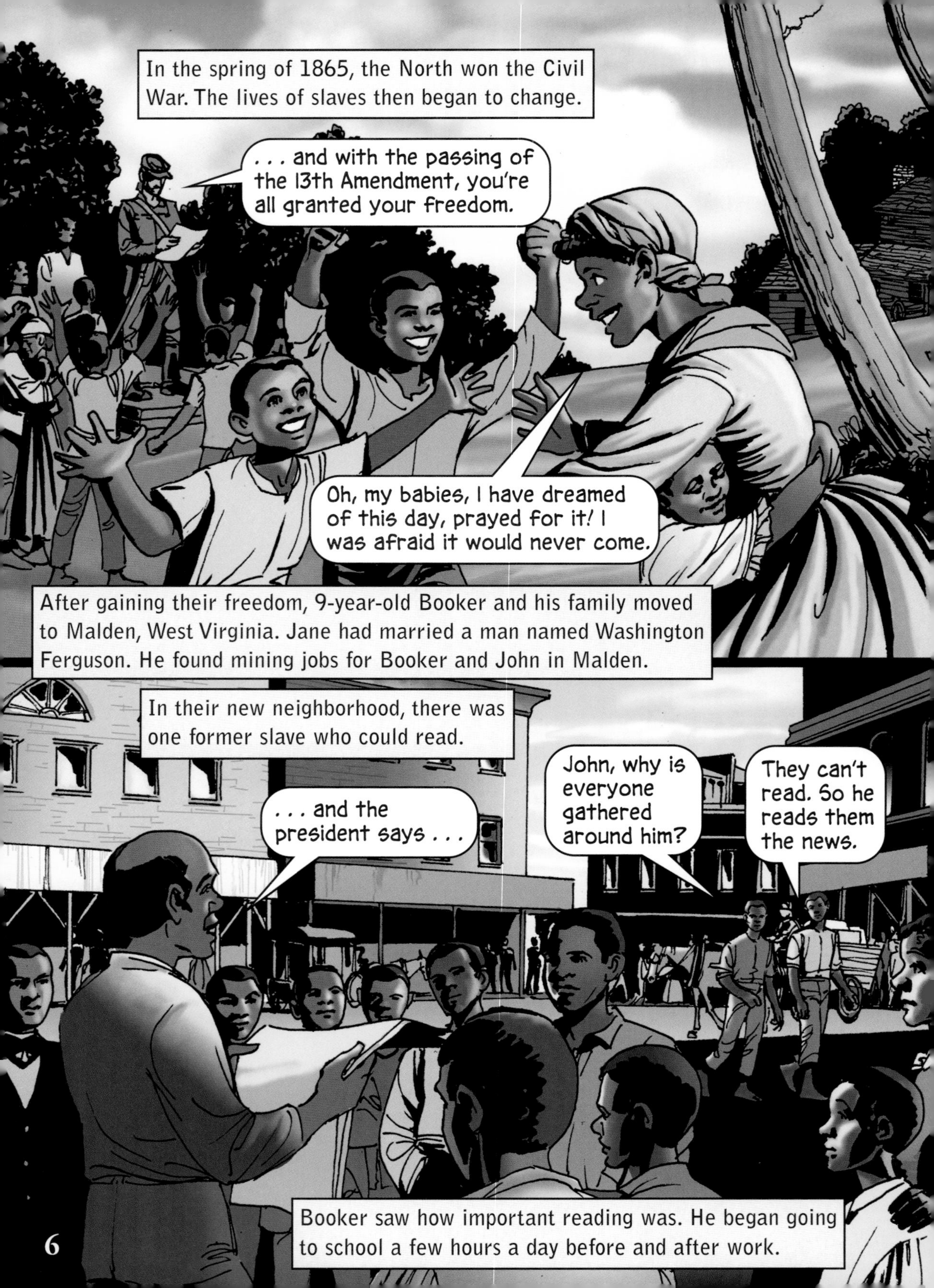
In the spring of 1865, the North won the Civil War. The lives of slaves then began to change.
. . . and with the passing of the 13th Amendment, you're all granted your freedom.
Oh, my babies, I have dreamed of this day, prayed for it! I was afraid it would never come.
After gaining their freedom, 9-year-old Booker and his family moved to Malden, West Virginia. Jane had married a man named Washington Ferguson. He found mining jobs for Booker and John in Malden.
In their new neighborhood, there was one former slave who could read.
. . . and the president says . . .
John, why is everyone gathered around him?
They can't read. So he reads them the news.
Booker saw how important reading was. He began going to school a few hours a day before and after work.

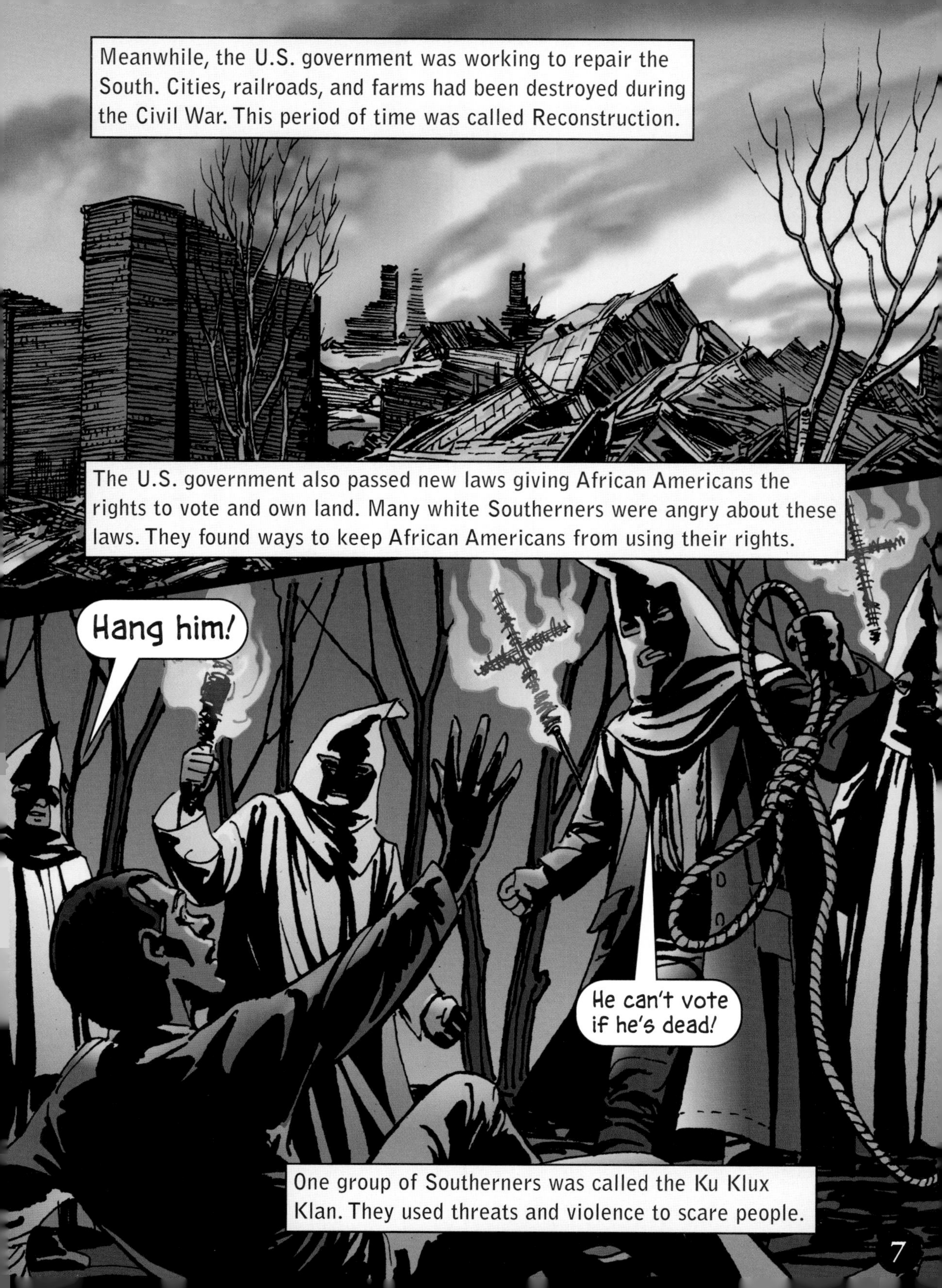
Meanwhile, the U.S. government was working to repair the South. Cities, railroads, and farms had been destroyed during the Civil War. This period of time was called Reconstruction.
The U.S. government also passed new laws giving African Americans the rights to vote and own land. Many white Southerners were angry about these laws. They found ways to keep African Americans from using their rights.
Hang him!
He can't vote if he's dead!
One group of Southerners was called the Ku Klux Klan. They used threats and violence to scare people.

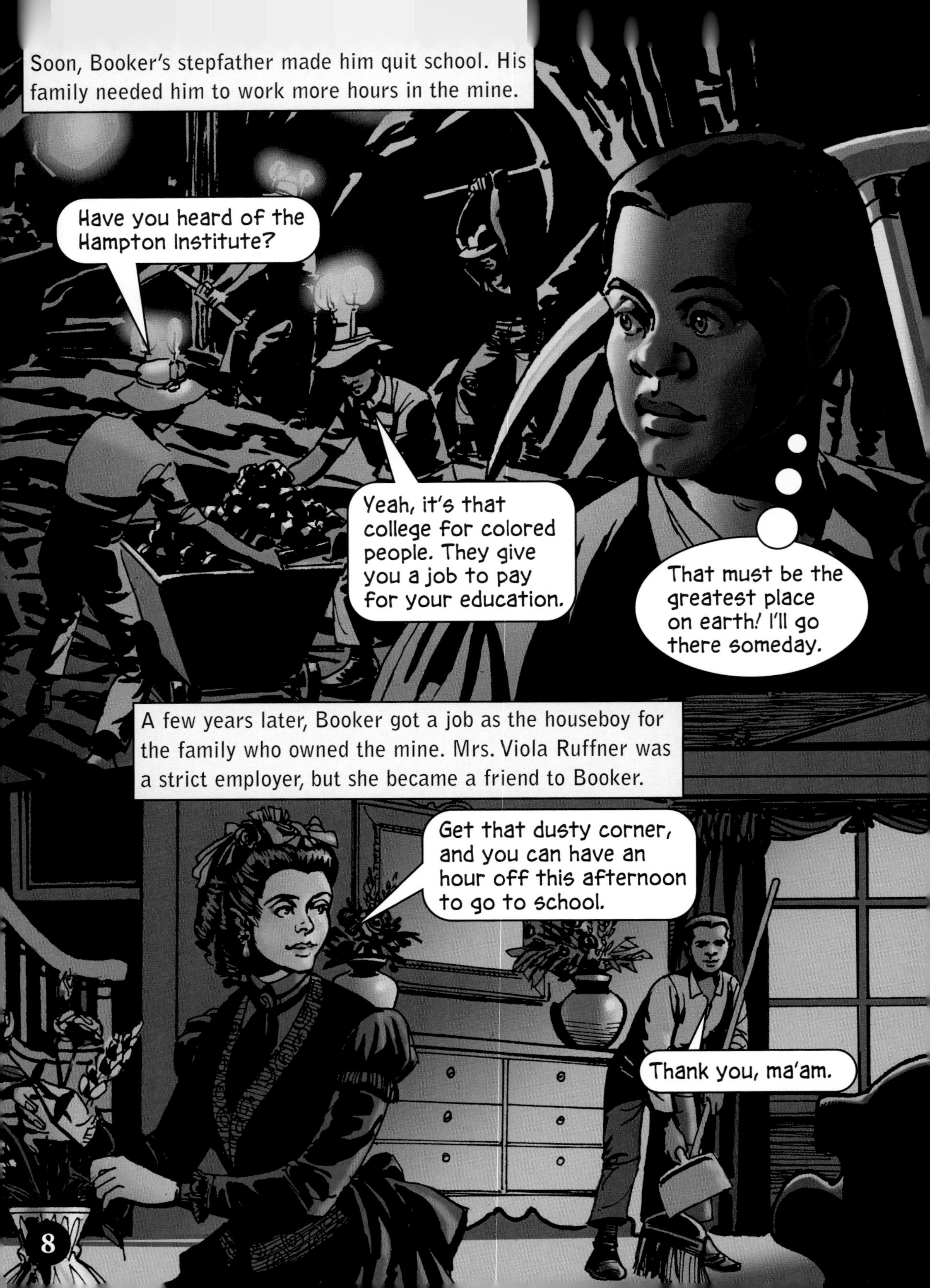
Soon, Booker's stepfather made him quit school. His family needed him to work more hours in the mine.
Have you heard of the Hampton Institute?
Yeah, it's that college for colored people. They give you a job to pay for your education.
That must be the greatest place on earth! I'll go there someday.
A few years later, Booker got a job as the houseboy for the family who owned the mine. Mrs. Viola Ruffner was a strict employer, but she became a friend to Booker.
Get that dusty corner, and you can have an hour off this afternoon to go to school.
Thank you, ma'am.

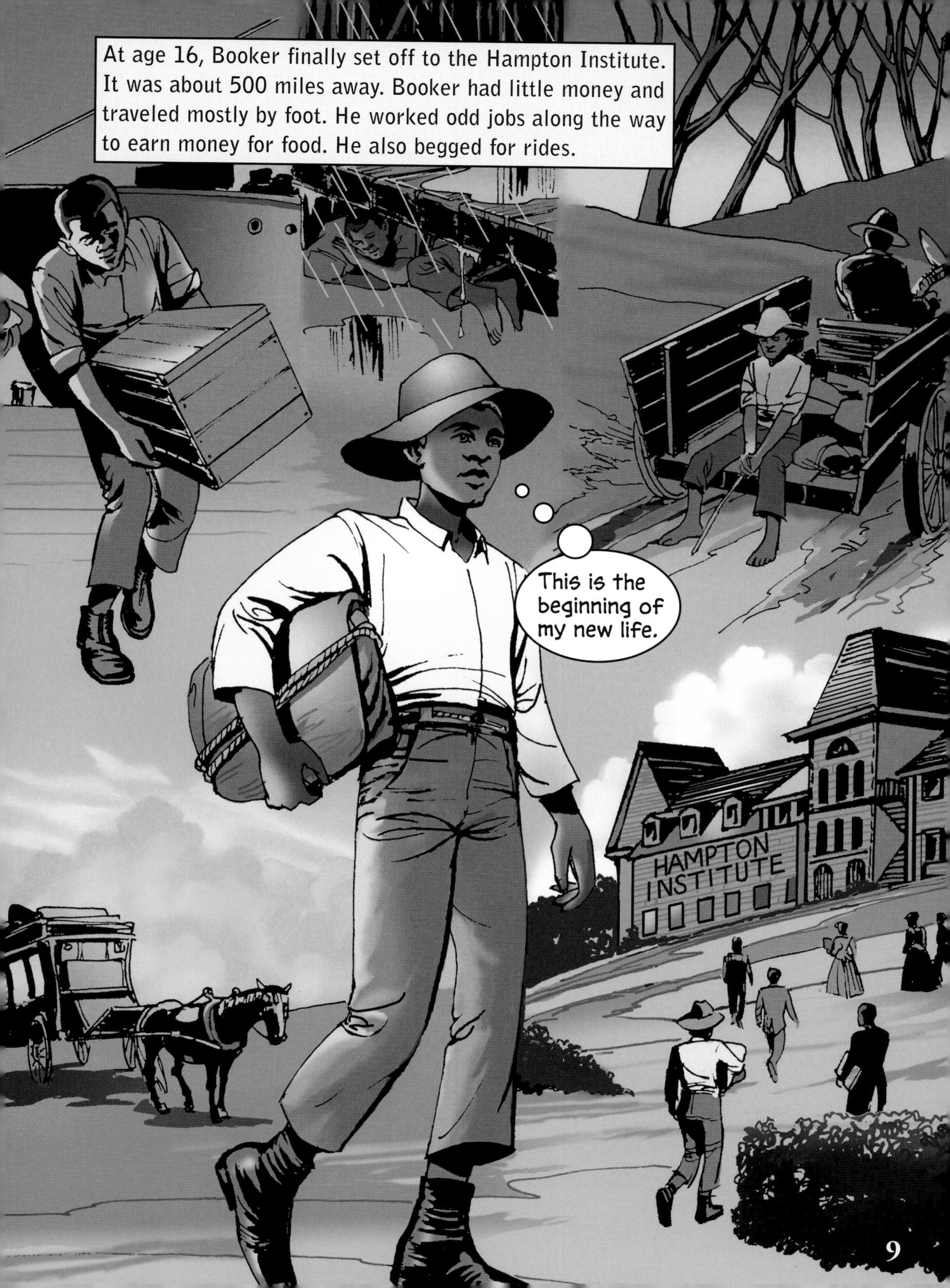
At age 16, Booker finally set off to the Hampton Institute. It was about 500 miles away. Booker had little money and traveled mostly by foot. He worked odd jobs along the way to earn money for food. He also begged for rides.
This is the beginning of my new life.
HAMPTON INSTITUTE

Chapter 2

The Importance of Education

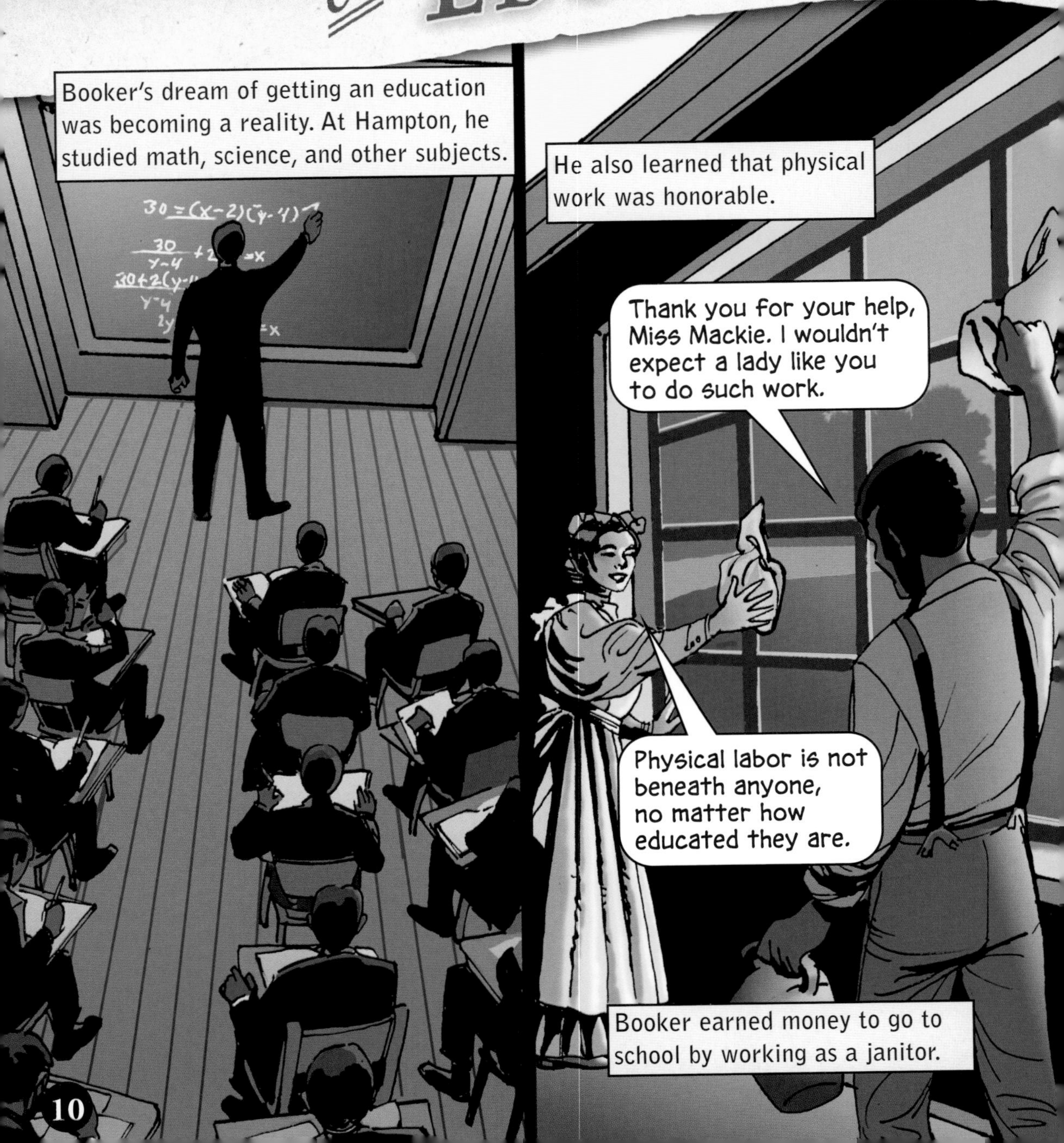
Booker's dream of getting an education was becoming a reality. At Hampton, he studied math, science, and other subjects.
He also learned that physical work was honorable.
Thank you for your help, Miss Mackie. I wouldn't expect a lady like you to do such work.
Physical labor is not beneath anyone, no matter how educated they are.
Booker earned money to go to school by working as a janitor.

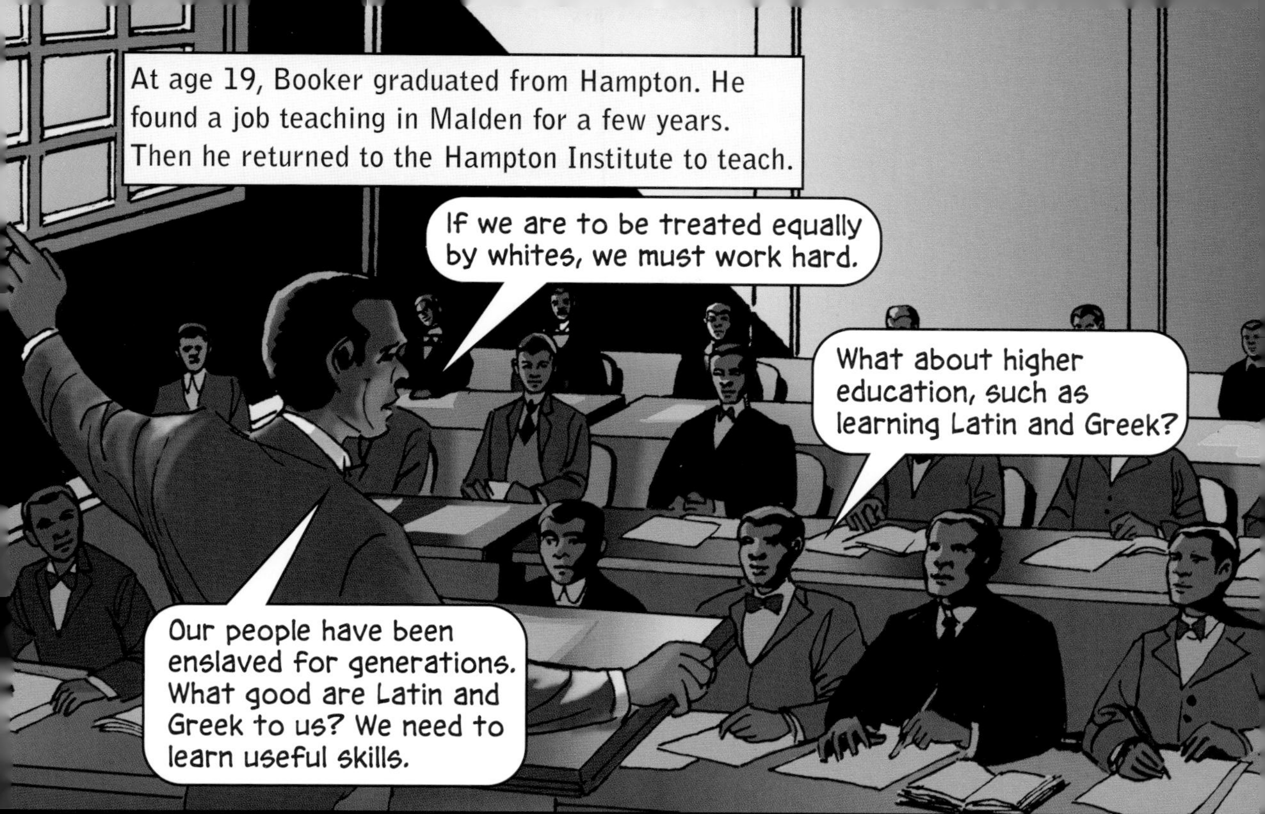
At age 19, Booker graduated from Hampton. He found a job teaching in Malden for a few years. Then he returned to the Hampton Institute to teach.
If we are to be treated equally by whites, we must work hard.
What about higher education, such as learning Latin and Greek?
Our people have been enslaved for generations. What good are Latin and Greek to us? We need to learn useful skills.

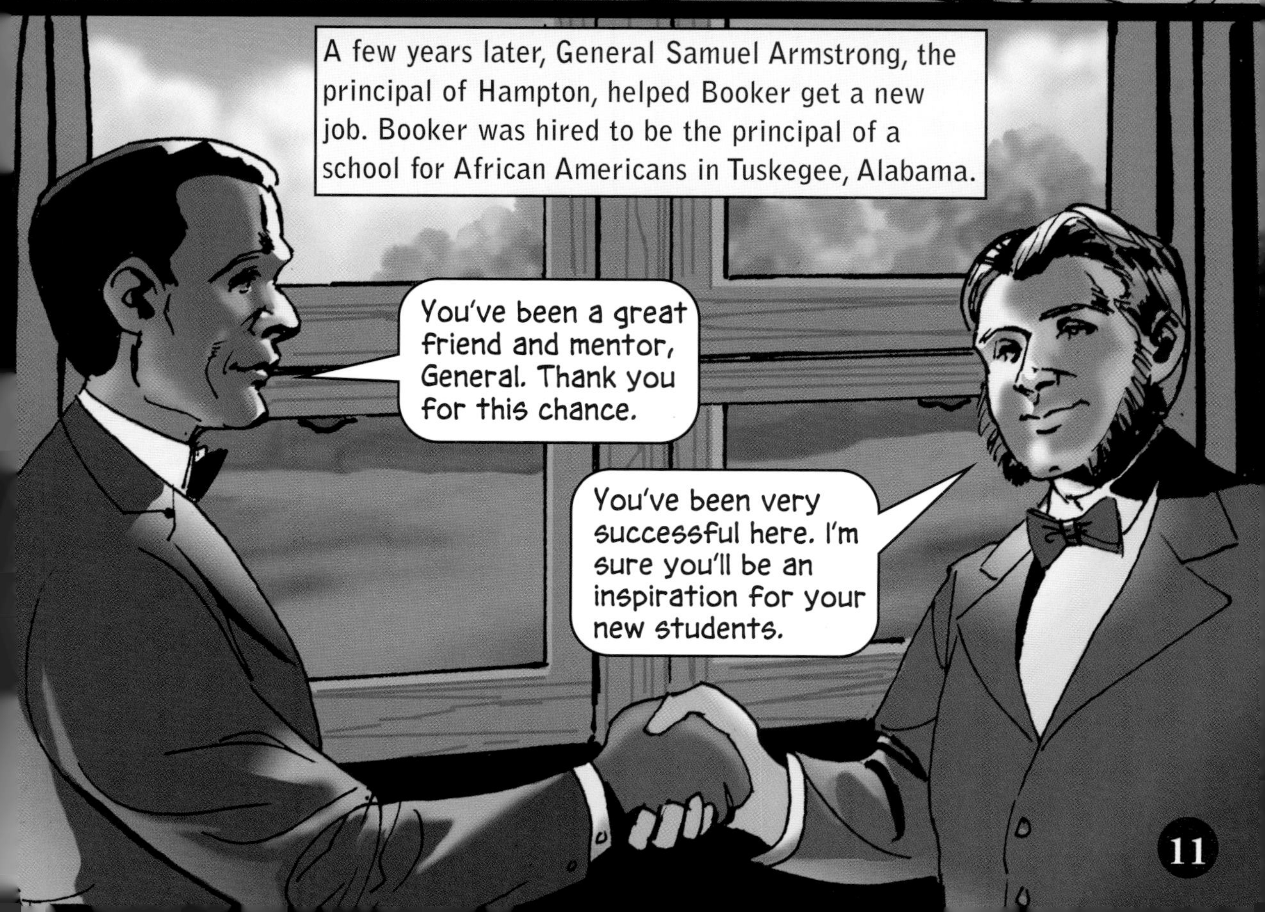
A few years later, General Samuel Armstrong, the principal of Hampton, helped Booker get a new job. Booker was hired to be the principal of a school for African Americans in Tuskegee, Alabama.
You've been a great friend and mentor, General. Thank you for this chance.
You've been very successful here. I'm sure you'll be an inspiration for your new students.

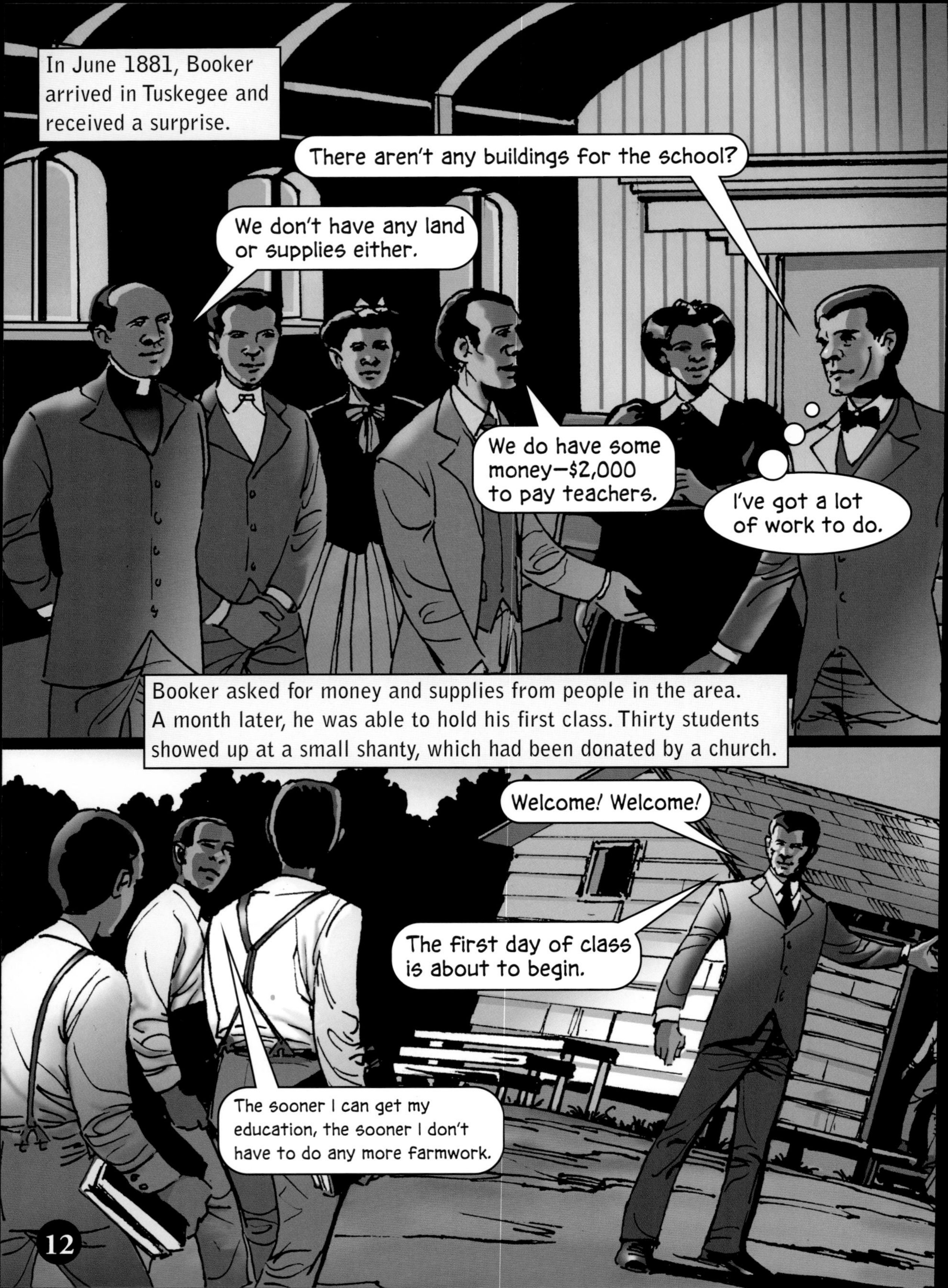
In June 1881, Booker arrived in Tuskegee and received a surprise.
There aren't any buildings for the school?
We don't have any land or supplies either.
We do have some money—$2,000 to pay teachers.
I've got a lot of work to do.
Booker asked for money and supplies from people in the area. A month later, he was able to hold his first class. Thirty students showed up at a small shanty, which had been donated by a church.
Welcome! Welcome!
The first day of class is about to begin.
The sooner I can get my education, the sooner I don't have to do any more farmwork.

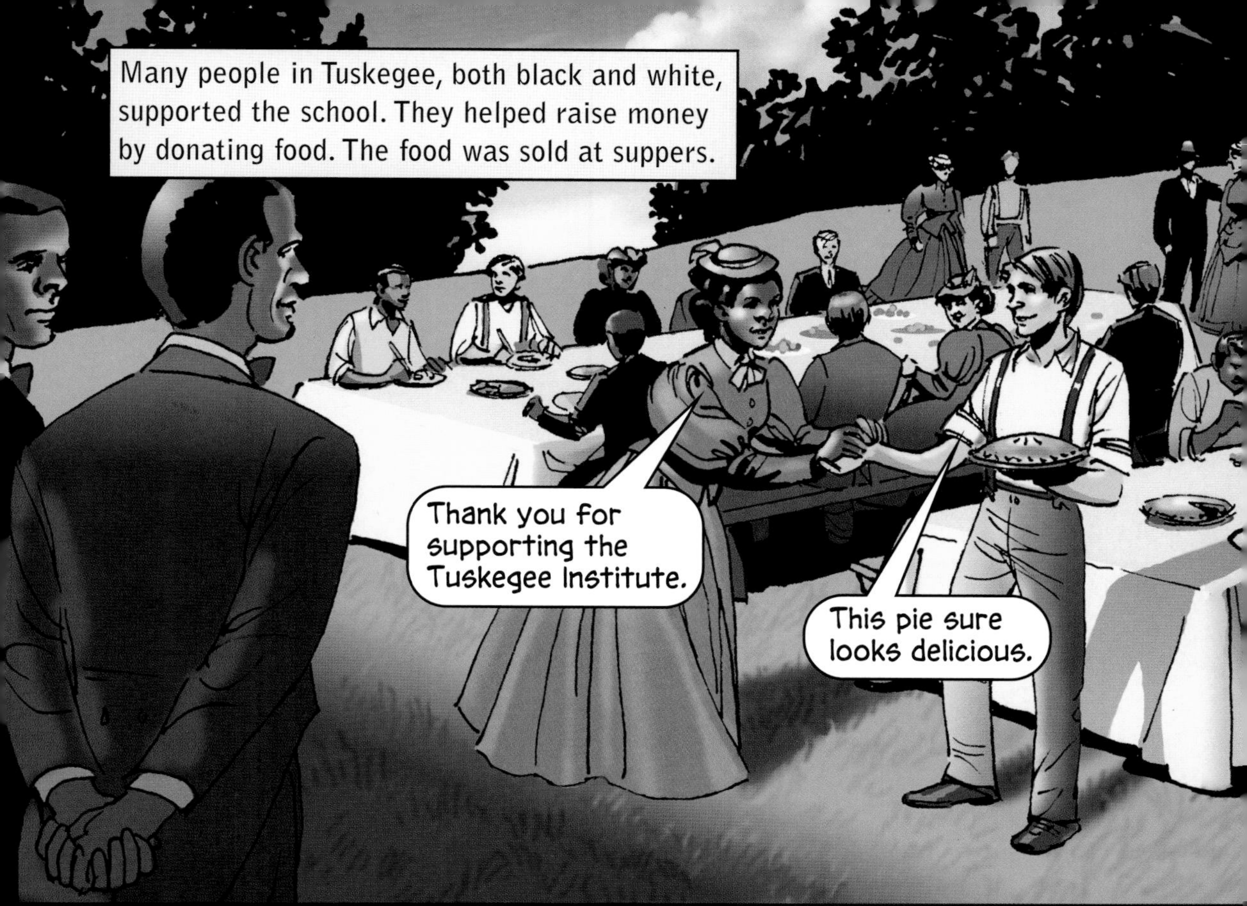
Many people in Tuskegee, both black and white, supported the school. They helped raise money by donating food. The food was sold at suppers.
Thank you for supporting the Tuskegee Institute.
This pie sure looks delicious.

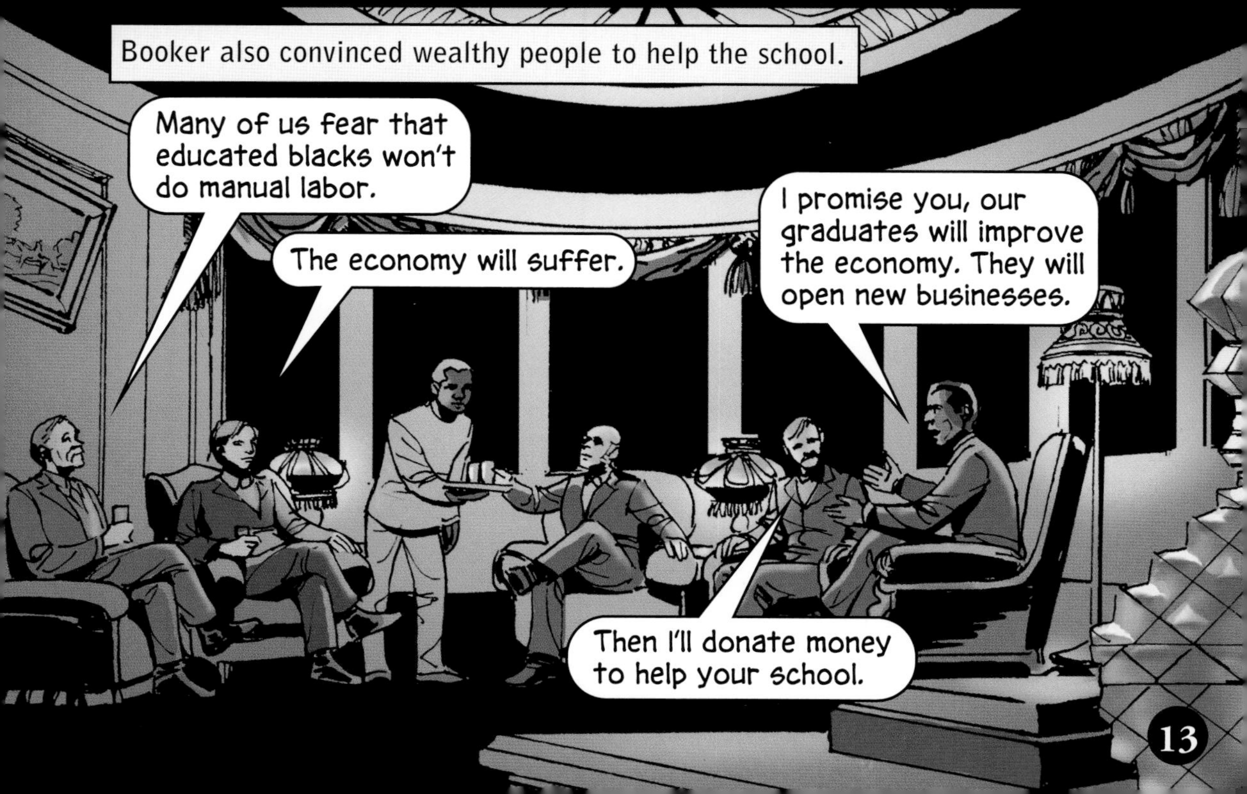
Booker also convinced wealthy people to help the school.
Many of us fear that educated blacks won't do manual labor.
The economy will suffer.
I promise you, our graduates will improve the economy. They will open new businesses.
Then I'll donate money to help your school.

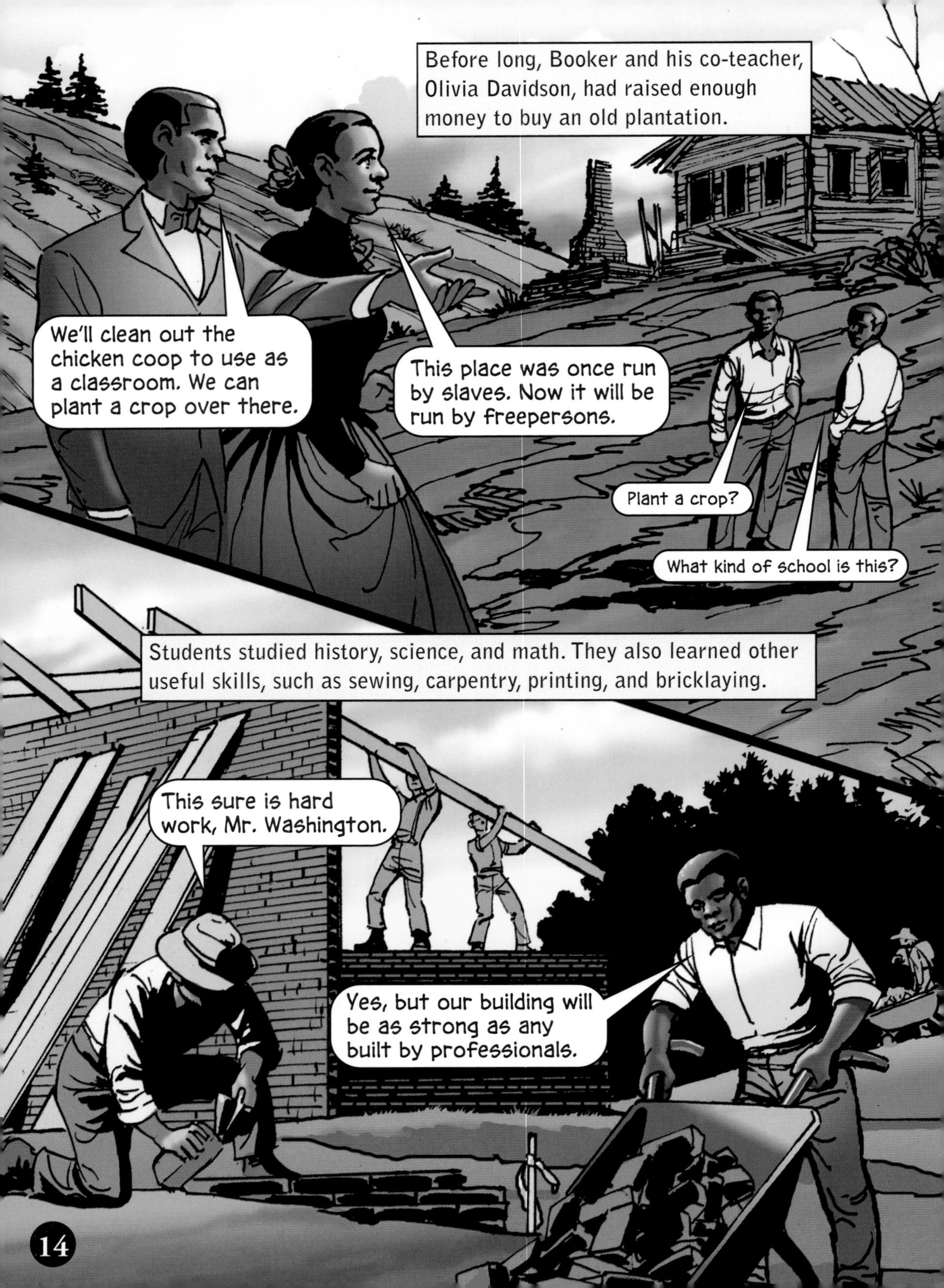
Before long, Booker and his co-teacher, Olivia Davidson, had raised enough money to buy an old plantation.
We'll clean out the chicken coop to use as a classroom. We can plant a crop over there.
This place was once run by slaves. Now it will be run by freepersons.
Plant a crop?
What kind of school is this?
Students studied history, science, and math. They also learned other useful skills, such as sewing, carpentry, printing, and bricklaying.
This sure is hard work, Mr. Washington.
Yes, but our building will be as strong as any built by professionals.

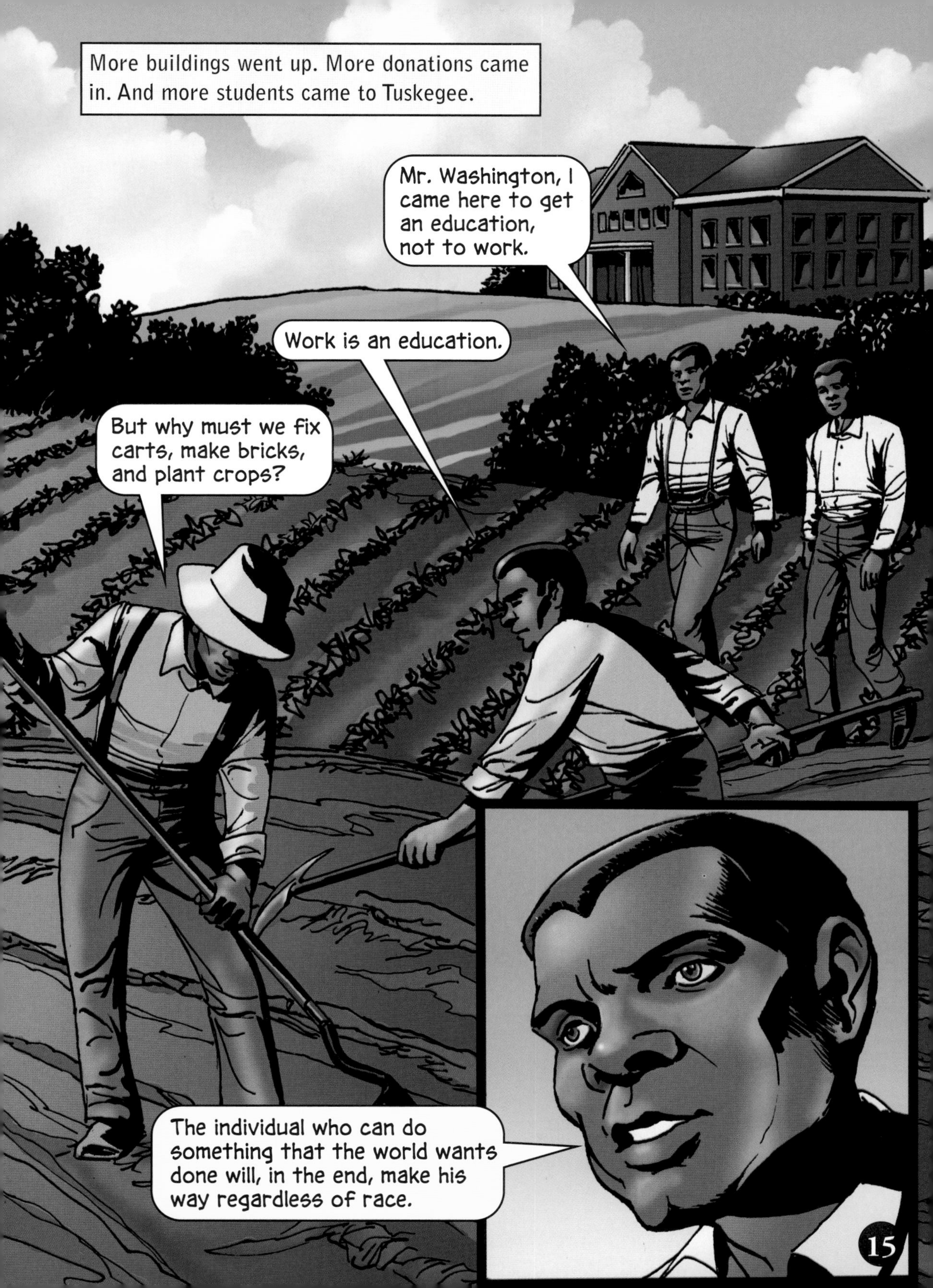
More buildings went up. More donations came in. And more students came to Tuskegee.
Mr. Washington, I came here to get an education, not to work.
Work is an education.
But why must we fix carts, make bricks, and plant crops?
The individual who can do something that the world wants done will, in the end, make his way regardless of race.

Chapter 3
Gaining Influence

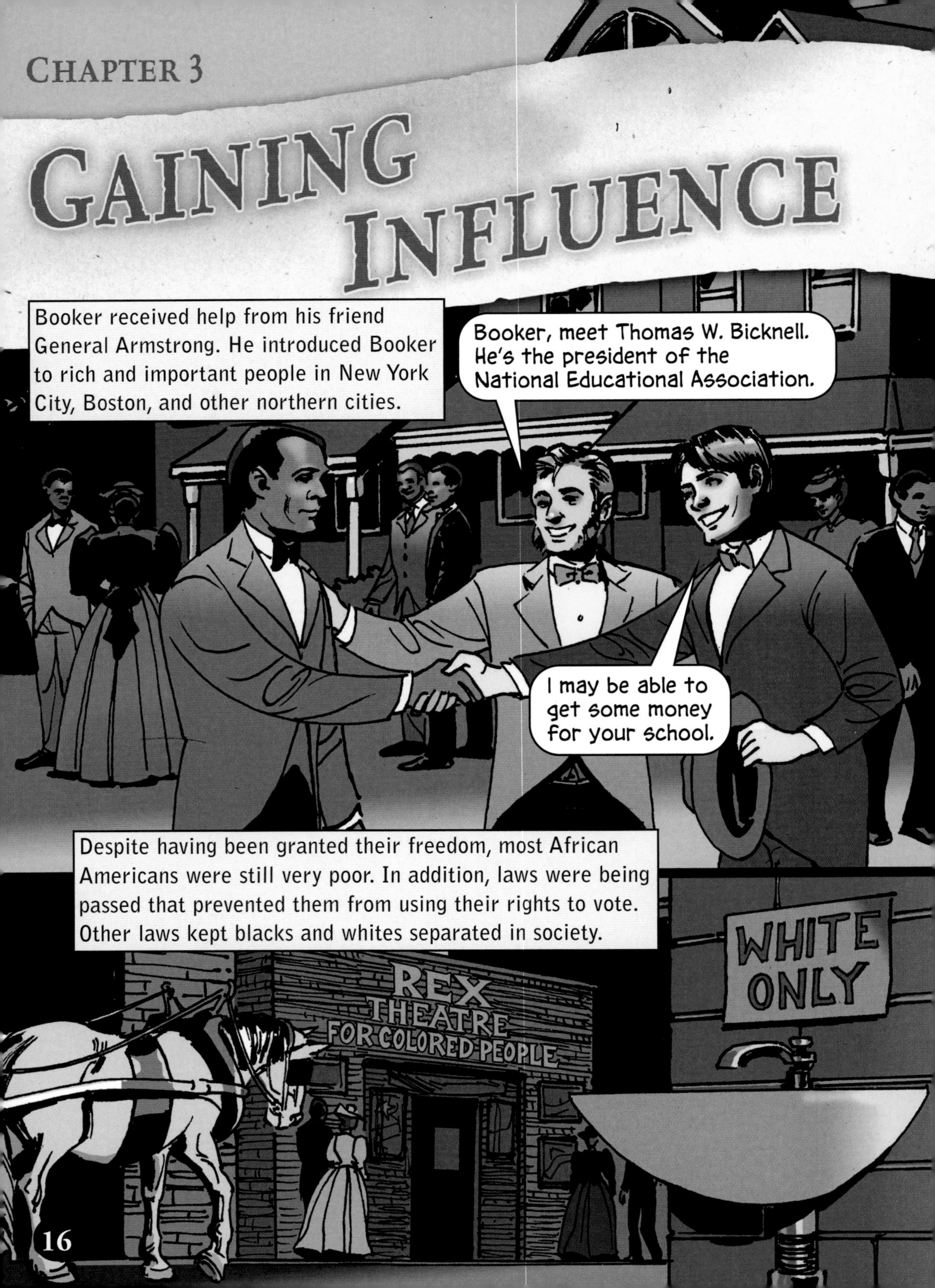
Booker received help from his friend General Armstrong. He introduced Booker to rich and important people in New York City, Boston, and other northern cities.
Booker, meet Thomas W. Bicknell. He's the president of the National Educational Association.
I may be able to get some money for your school.
Despite having been granted their freedom, most African Americans were still very poor. In addition, laws were being passed that prevented them from using their rights to vote. Other laws kept blacks and whites separated in society.
REX THEATRE FOR COLORED PEOPLE
WHITE ONLY

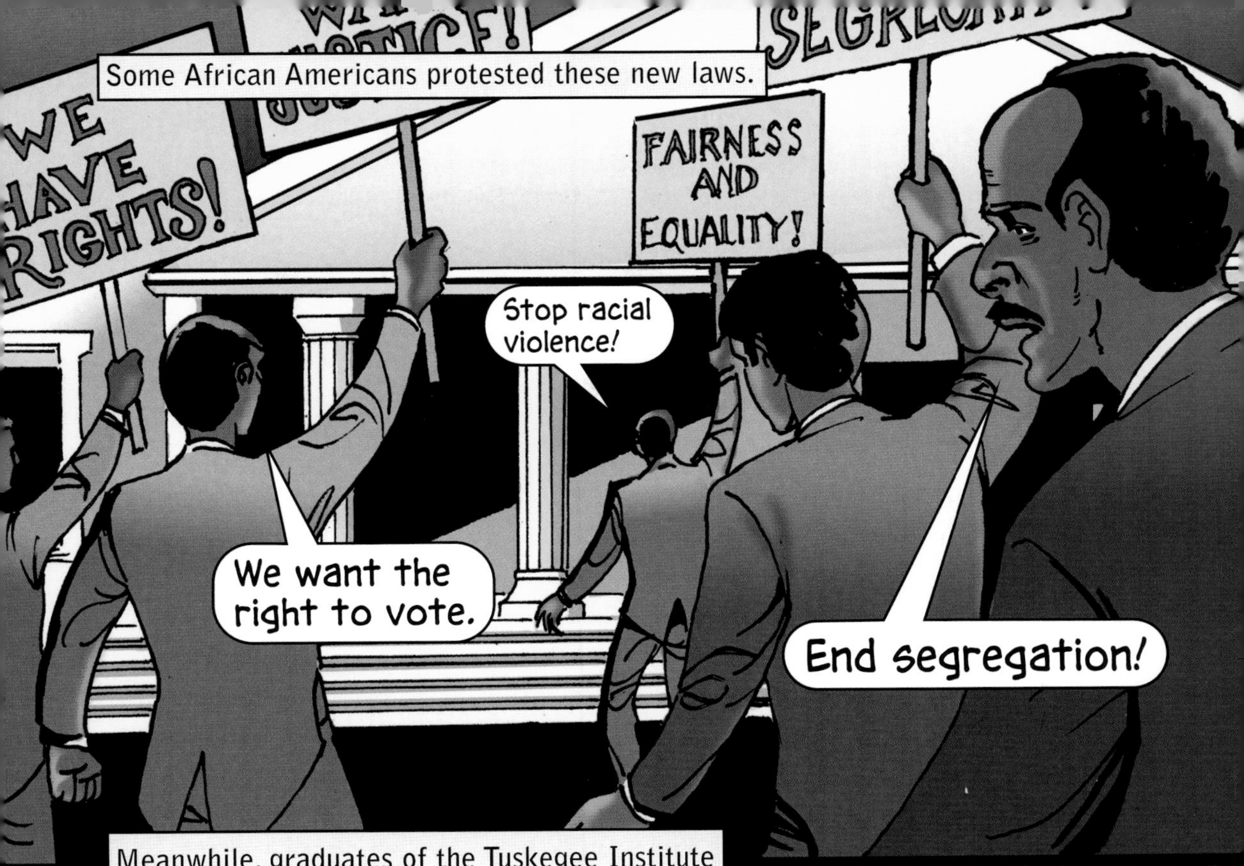
Some African Americans protested these new laws.
FAIRNESS AND EQUALITY!
Stop racial violence!
We want the right to vote.
End segregation!

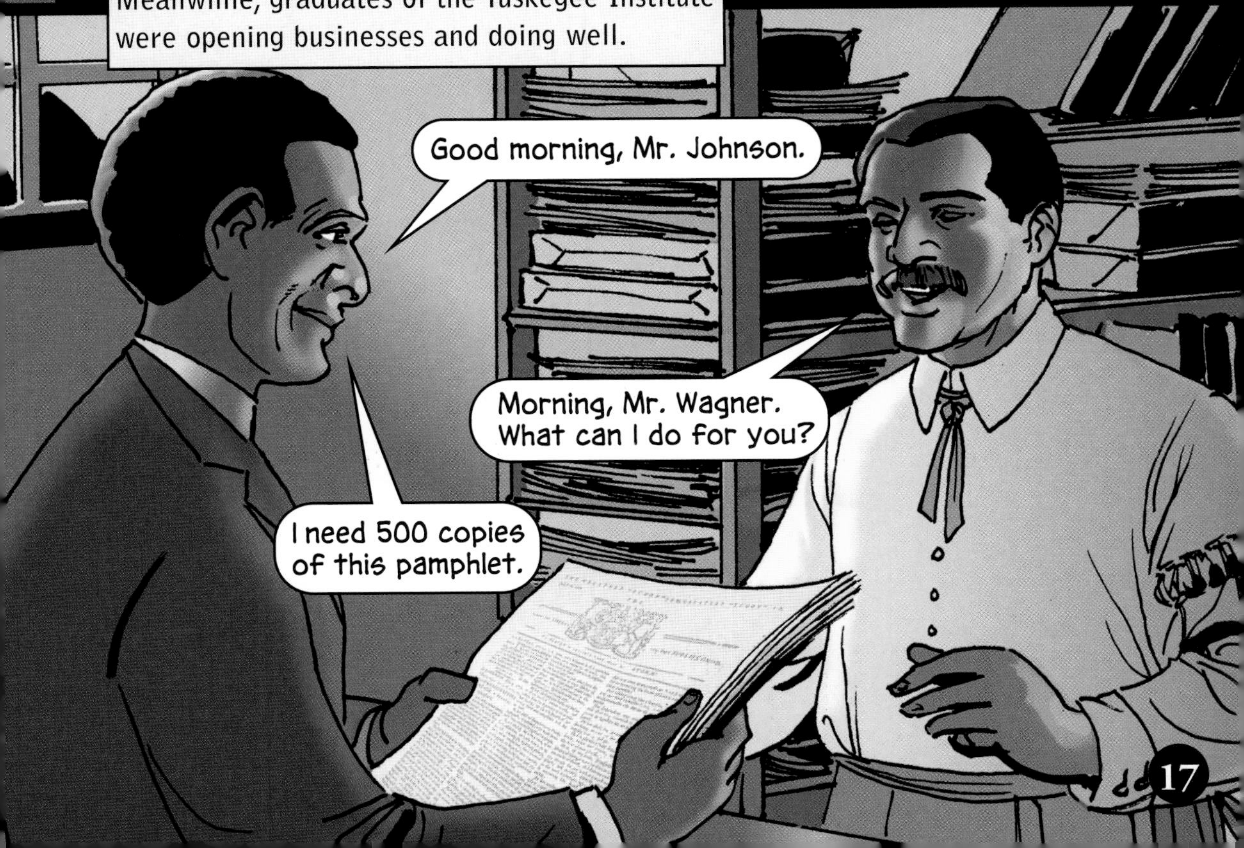
Meanwhile, graduates of the Tuskegee Institute were opening businesses and doing well.
Good morning, Mr. Johnson.
Morning, Mr. Wagner. What can I do for you?
I need 500 copies of this pamphlet.

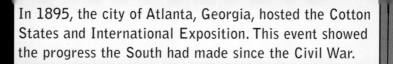

In 1895, the city of Atlanta, Georgia, hosted the Cotton States and International Exposition. This event showed the progress the South had made since the Civil War.

The Tuskegee exhibit is the most popular one here!

I am surprised to see how well their students have done.

Booker gave a speech at the exposition. He spoke about the state of the African American race and its future.

Our greatest danger is that in the great leap from slavery to freedom we may overlook the fact that masses of us are to live by the productions of our hands.

No race can prosper until it learns that there is as much dignity in tilling a field as in writing a poem.

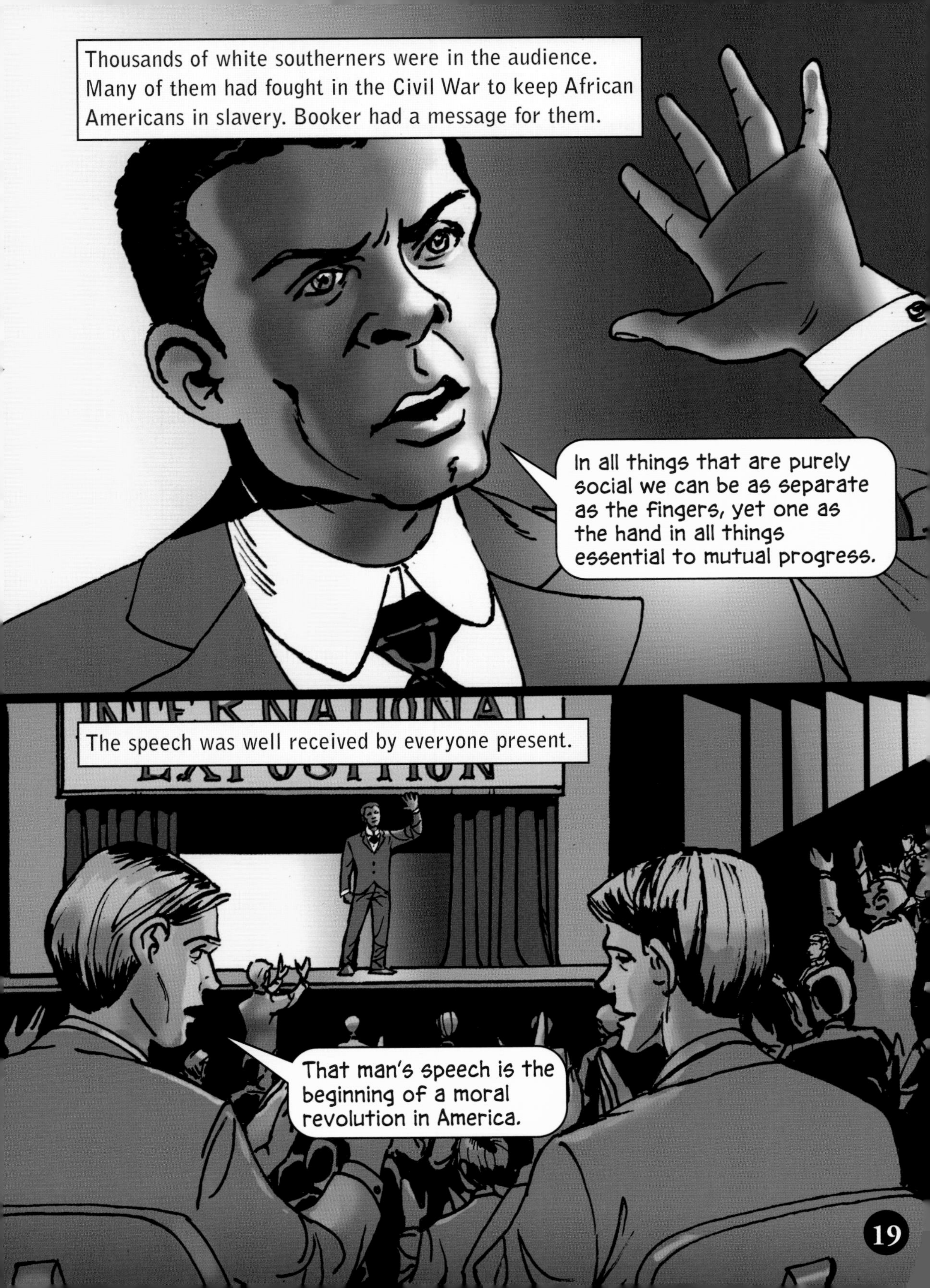
Thousands of white southerners were in the audience. Many of them had fought in the Civil War to keep African Americans in slavery. Booker had a message for them.
In all things that are purely social we can be as separate as the fingers, yet one as the hand in all things essential to mutual progress.
The speech was well received by everyone present.
That man's speech is the beginning of a moral revolution in America.

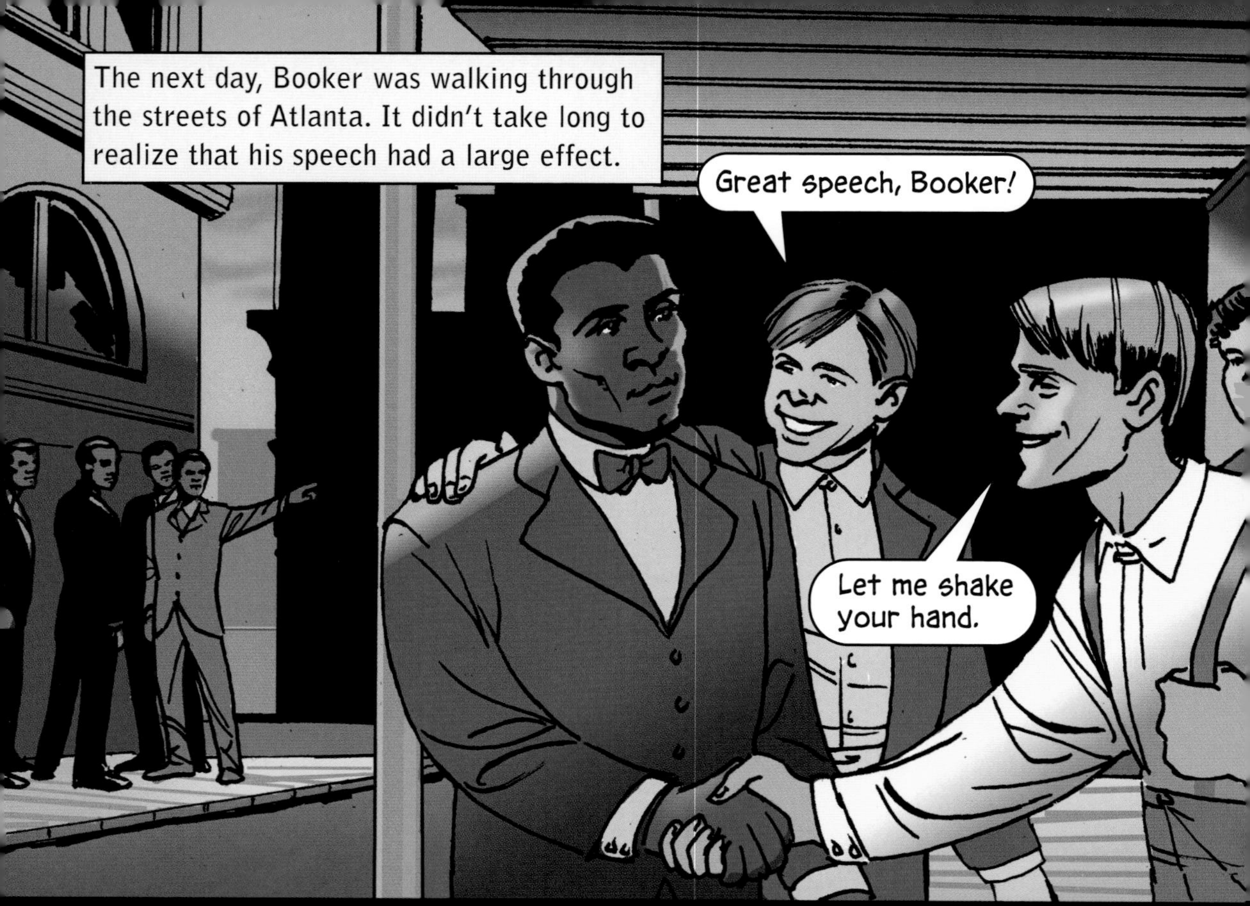
The next day, Booker was walking through the streets of Atlanta. It didn't take long to realize that his speech had a large effect.
Great speech, Booker!
Let me shake your hand.

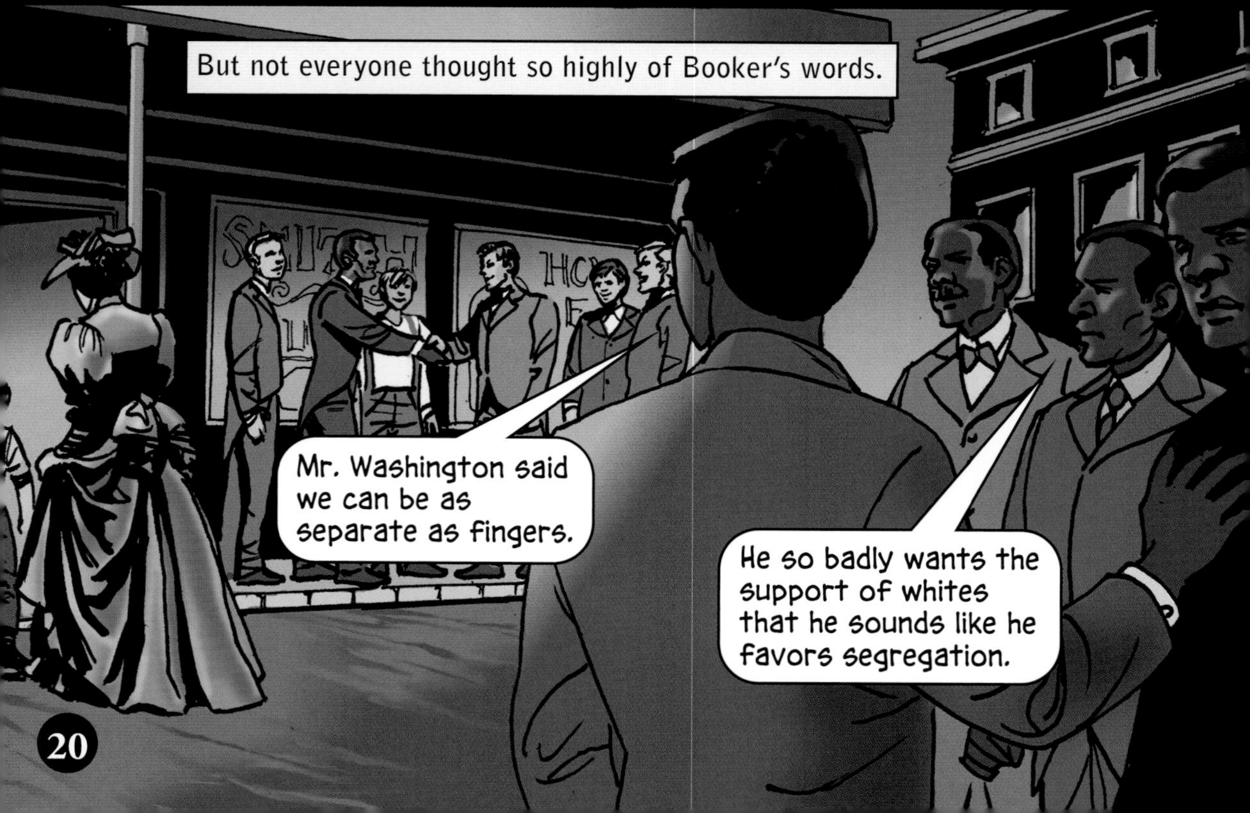
But not everyone thought so highly of Booker's words.
Mr. Washington said we can be as separate as fingers.
He so badly wants the support of whites that he sounds like he favors segregation.

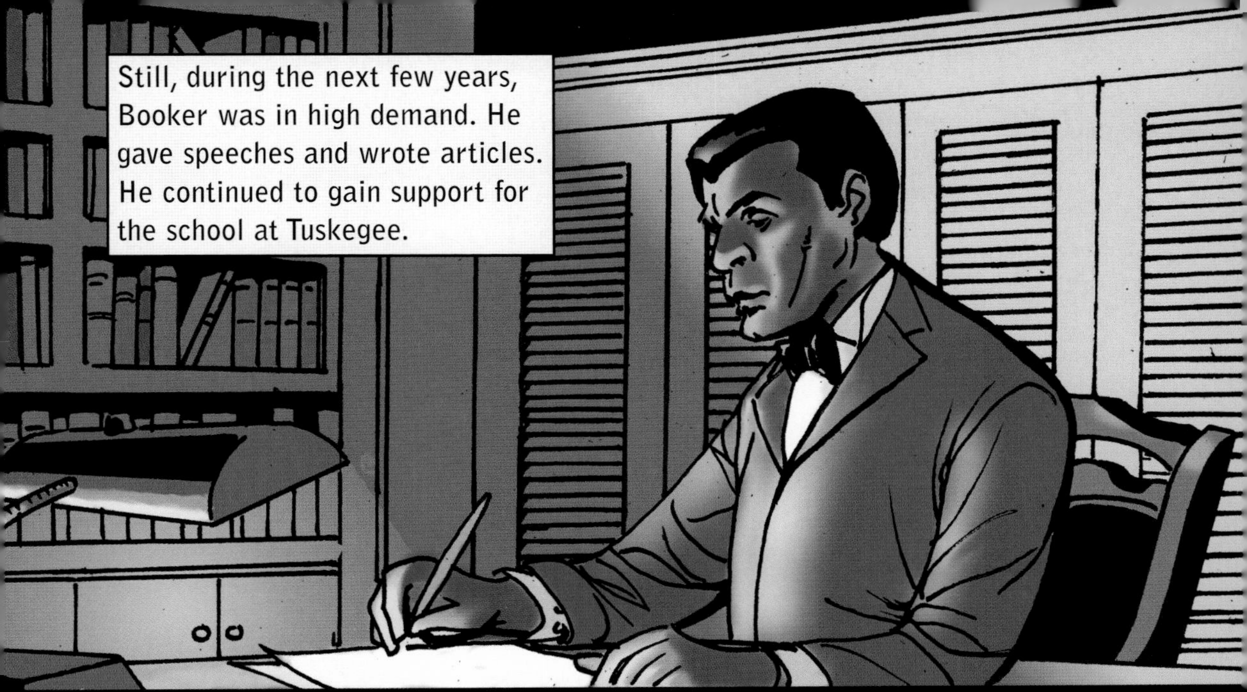
Still, during the next few years, Booker was in high demand. He gave speeches and wrote articles. He continued to gain support for the school at Tuskegee.

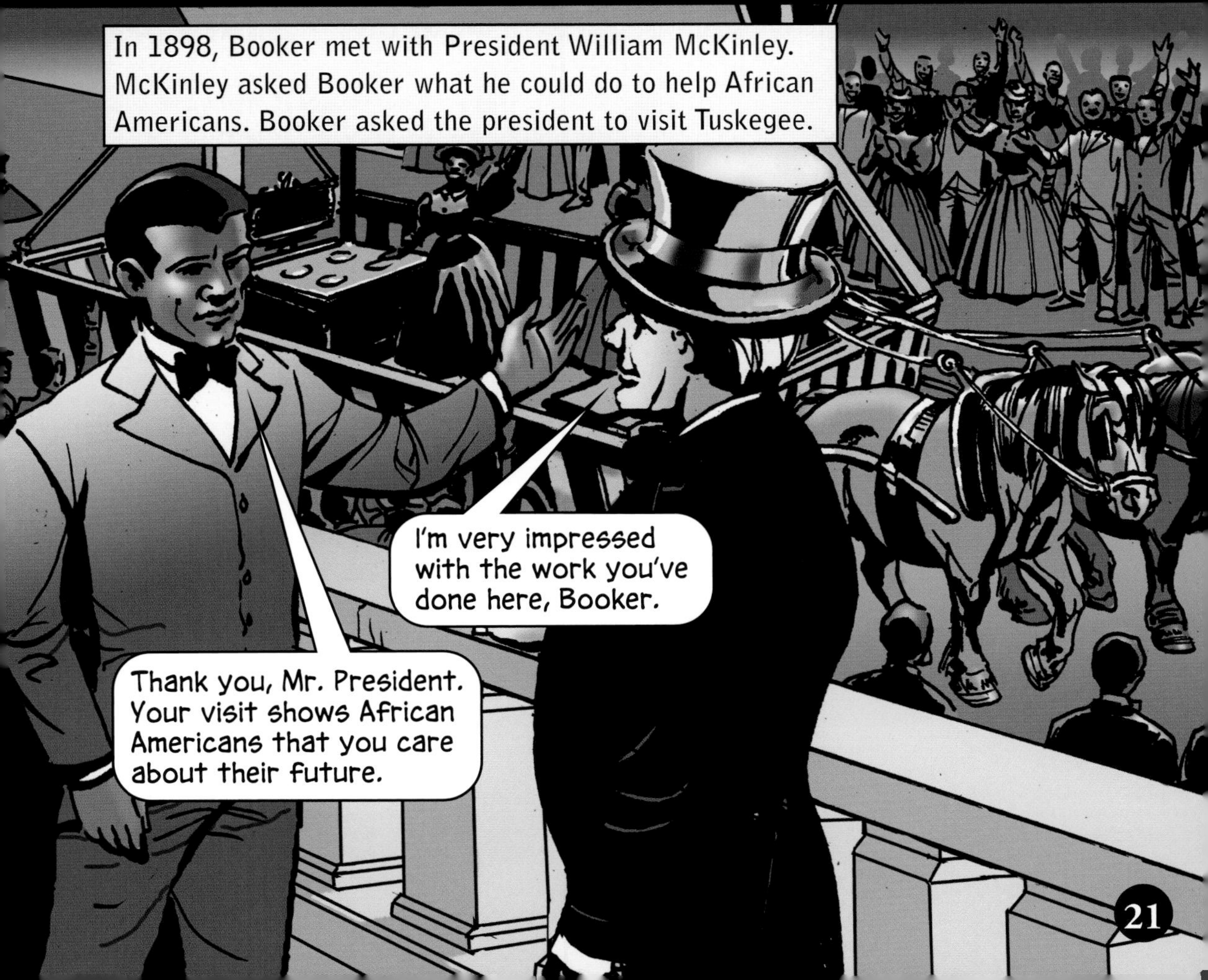
In 1898, Booker met with President William McKinley. McKinley asked Booker what he could do to help African Americans. Booker asked the president to visit Tuskegee.
I'm very impressed with the work you've done here, Booker.
Thank you, Mr. President. Your visit shows African Americans that you care about their future.

CHAPTER 4

THE QUESTION OF RACE

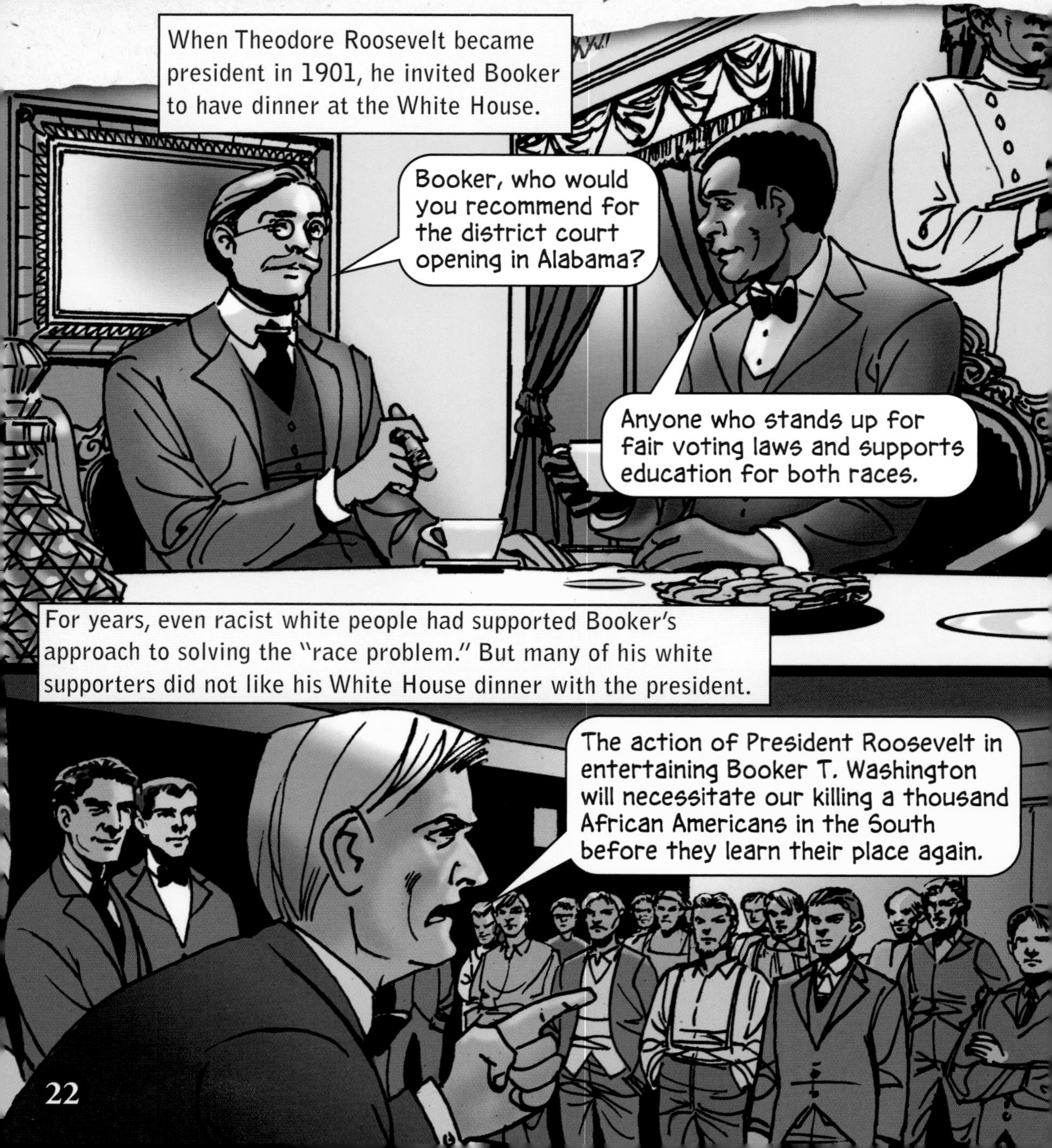
When Theodore Roosevelt became president in 1901, he invited Booker to have dinner at the White House.
Booker, who would you recommend for the district court opening in Alabama?
Anyone who stands up for fair voting laws and supports education for both races.
For years, even racist white people had supported Booker's approach to solving the "race problem." But many of his white supporters did not like his White House dinner with the president.
The action of President Roosevelt in entertaining Booker T. Washington will necessitate our killing a thousand African Americans in the South before they learn their place again.

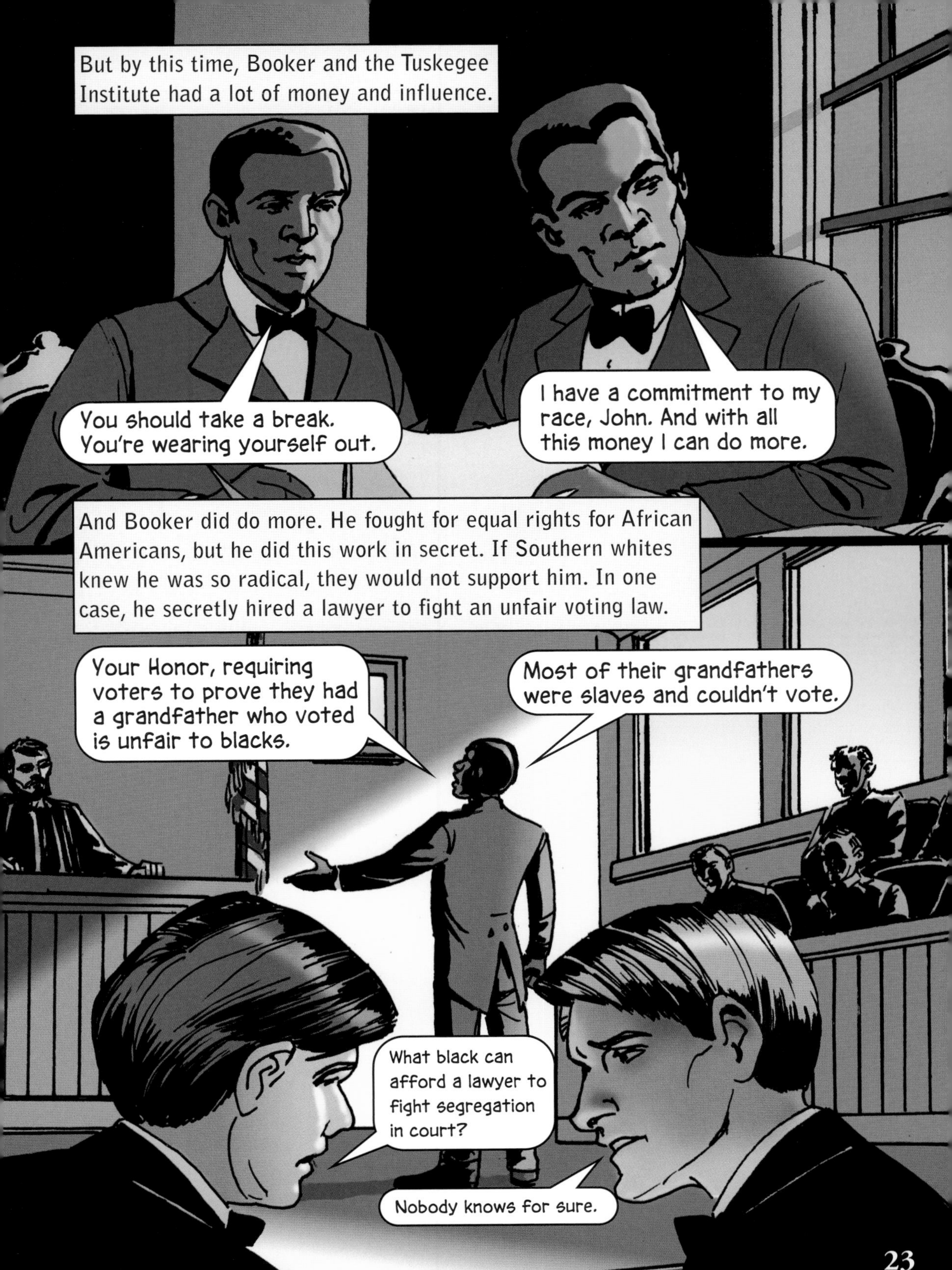
But by this time, Booker and the Tuskegee Institute had a lot of money and influence.
You should take a break. You're wearing yourself out.
I have a commitment to my race, John. And with all this money I can do more.
And Booker did do more. He fought for equal rights for African Americans, but he did this work in secret. If Southern whites knew he was so radical, they would not support him. In one case, he secretly hired a lawyer to fight an unfair voting law.
Your Honor, requiring voters to prove they had a grandfather who voted is unfair to blacks.
Most of their grandfathers were slaves and couldn't vote.
What black can afford a lawyer to fight segregation in court?
Nobody knows for sure.

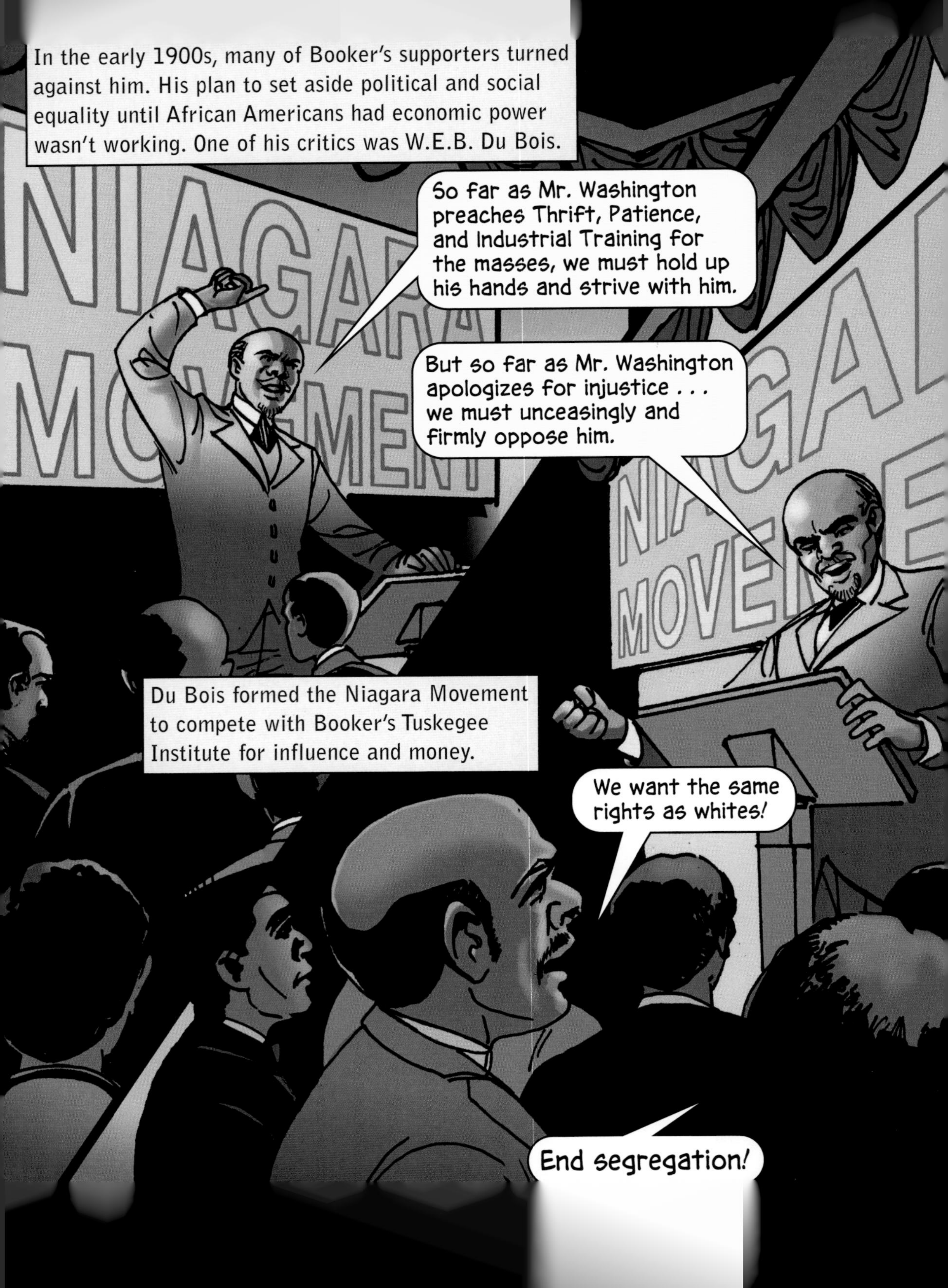

In the early 1900s, many of Booker's supporters turned against him. His plan to set aside political and social equality until African Americans had economic power wasn't working. One of his critics was W.E.B. Du Bois.
NIAGARA MOVEMENT
So far as Mr. Washington preaches Thrift, Patience, and Industrial Training for the masses, we must hold up his hands and strive with him.
But so far as Mr. Washington apologizes for injustice . . . we must unceasingly and firmly oppose him.
Du Bois formed the Niagara Movement to compete with Booker's Tuskegee Institute for influence and money.
We want the same rights as whites!
End segregation!

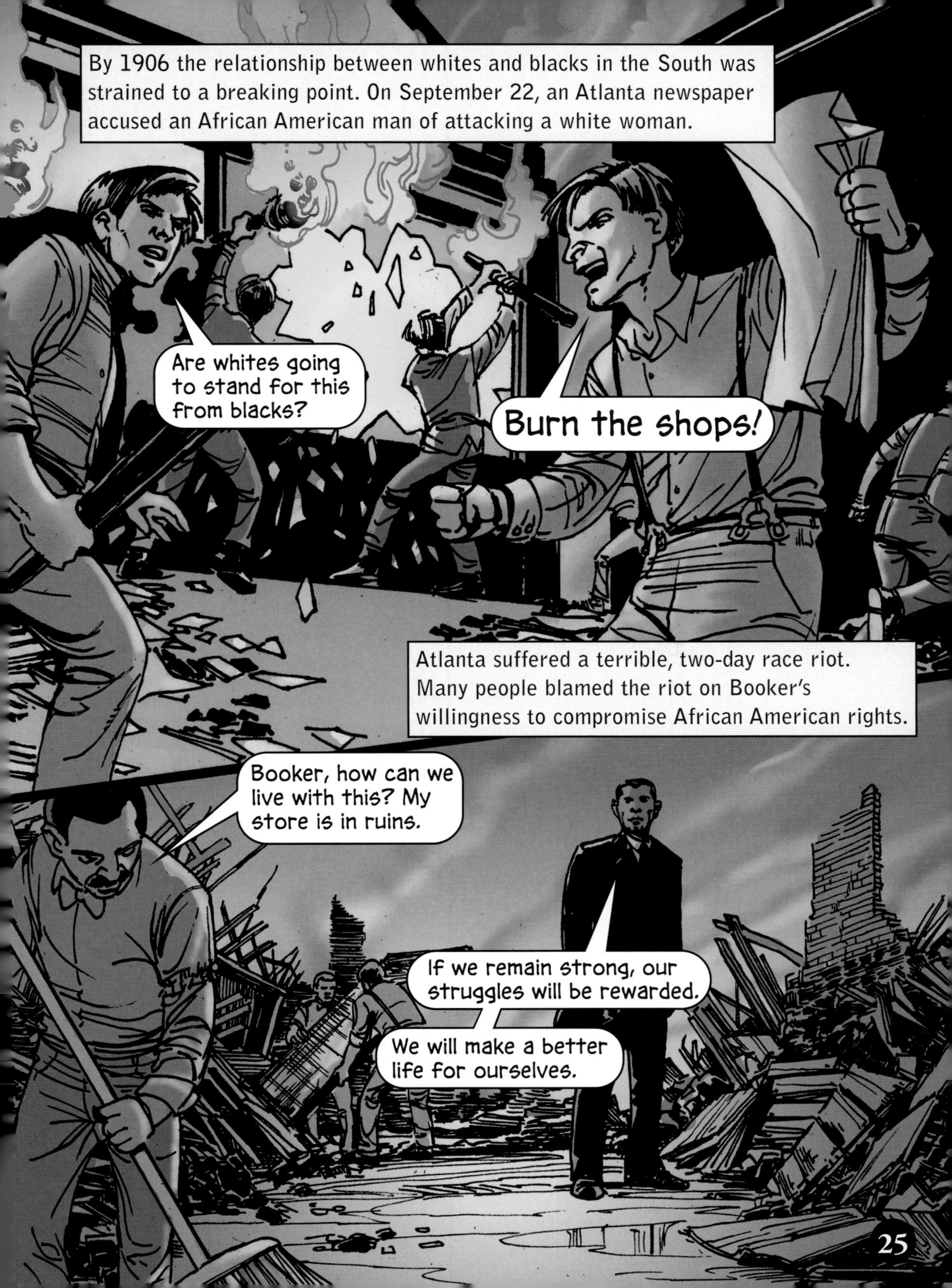
By 1906 the relationship between whites and blacks in the South was strained to a breaking point. On September 22, an Atlanta newspaper accused an African American man of attacking a white woman.
Are whites going to stand for this from blacks?
Burn the shops!
Atlanta suffered a terrible, two-day race riot. Many people blamed the riot on Booker's willingness to compromise African American rights.
Booker, how can we live with this? My store is in ruins.
If we remain strong, our struggles will be rewarded.
We will make a better life for ourselves.

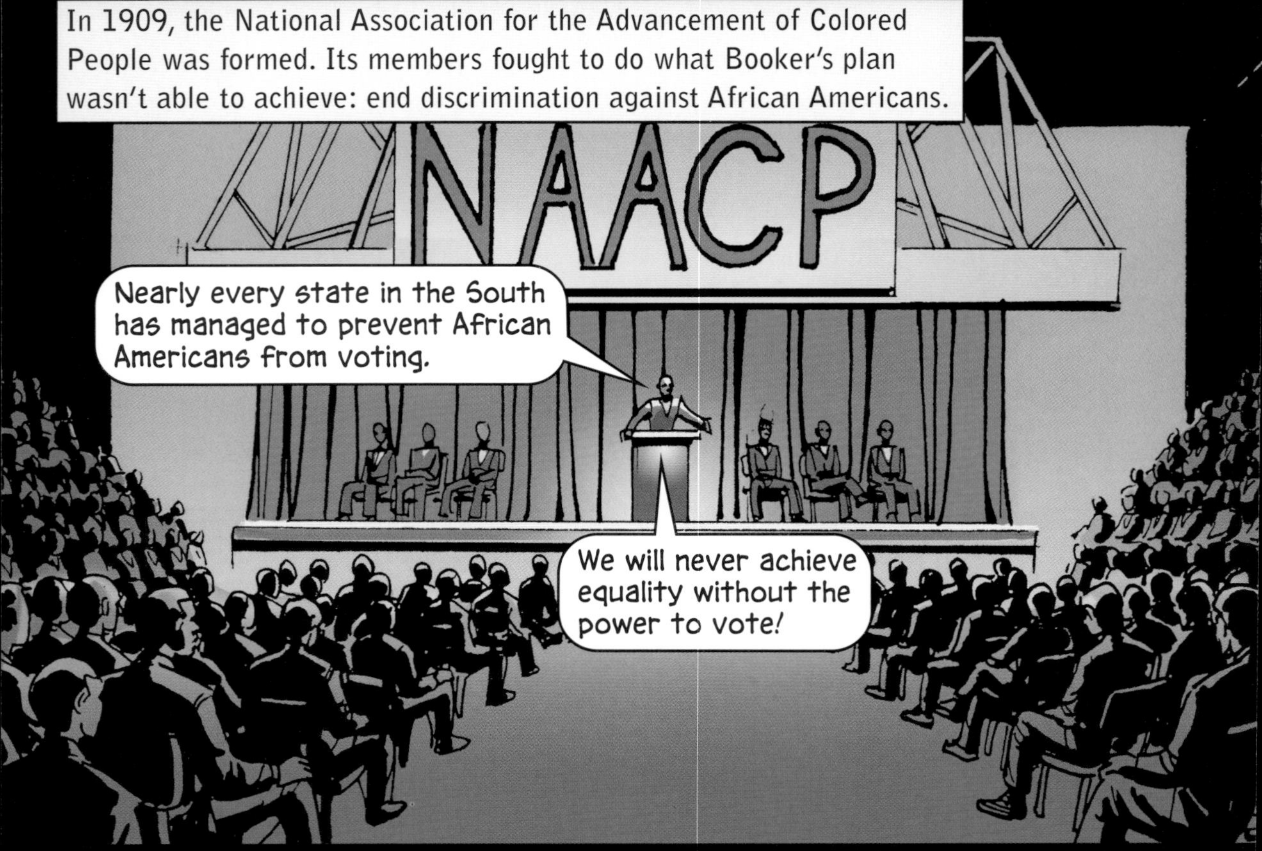
In 1909, the National Association for the Advancement of Colored People was formed. Its members fought to do what Booker's plan wasn't able to achieve: end discrimination against African Americans.
NAACP
Nearly every state in the South has managed to prevent African Americans from voting.
We will never achieve equality without the power to vote!

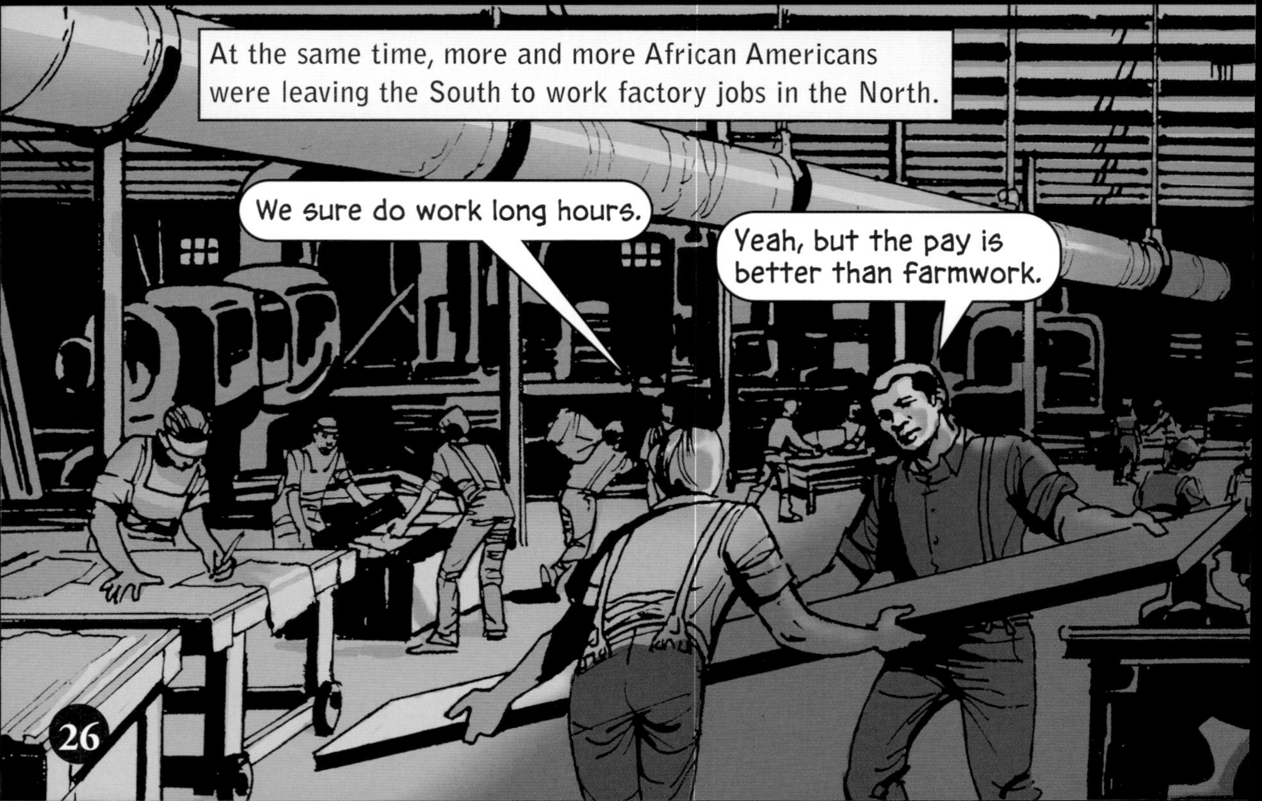
At the same time, more and more African Americans were leaving the South to work factory jobs in the North.
We sure do work long hours.
Yeah, but the pay is better than farmwork.

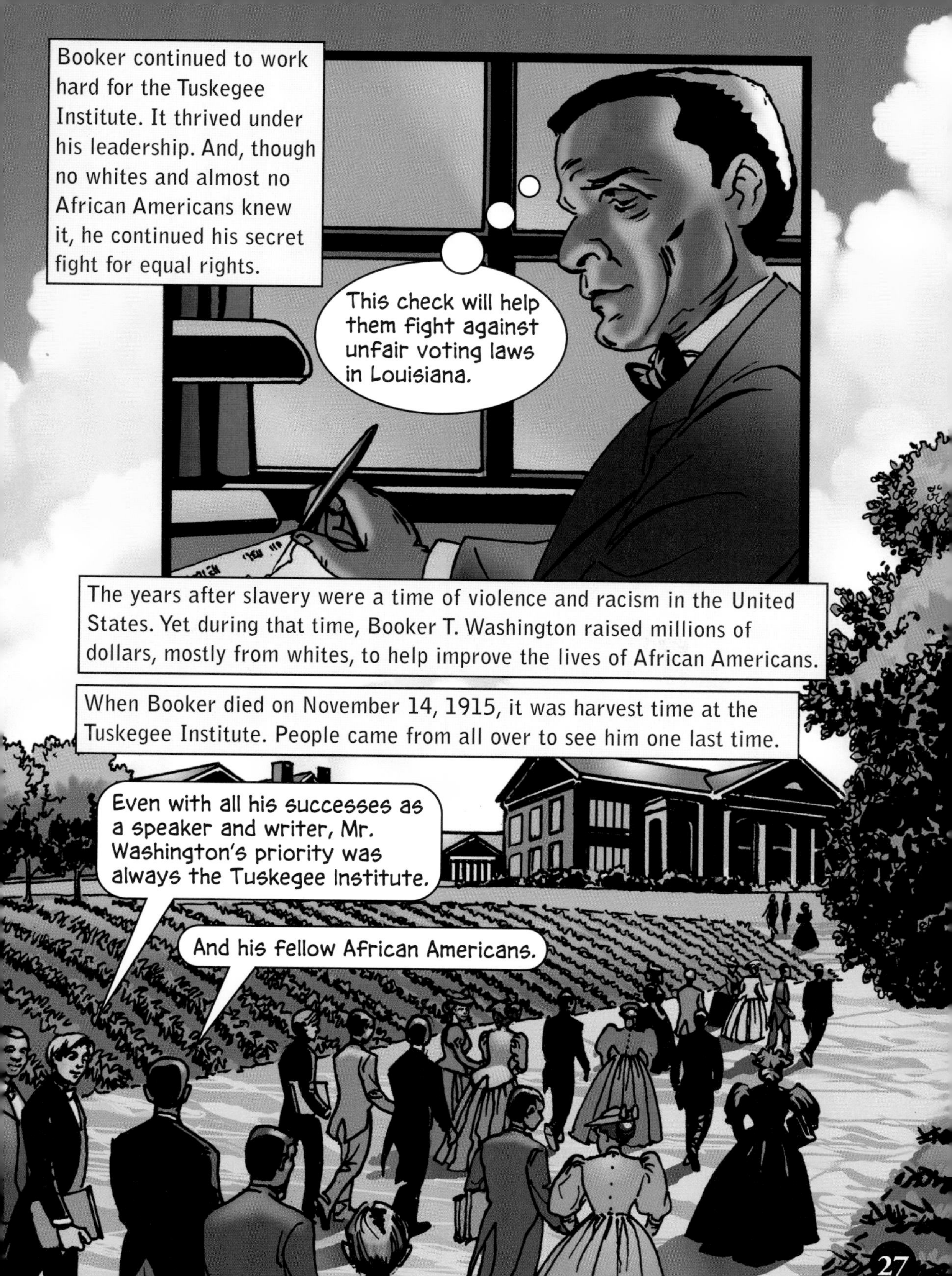
Booker continued to work hard for the Tuskegee Institute. It thrived under his leadership. And, though no whites and almost no African Americans knew it, he continued his secret fight for equal rights.
This check will help them fight against unfair voting laws in Louisiana.
The years after slavery were a time of violence and racism in the United States. Yet during that time, Booker T. Washington raised millions of dollars, mostly from whites, to help improve the lives of African Americans.
When Booker died on November 14, 1915, it was harvest time at the Tuskegee Institute. People came from all over to see him one last time.
Even with all his successes as a speaker and writer, Mr. Washington's priority was always the Tuskegee Institute.
And his fellow African Americans.

More About Booker T. Washington

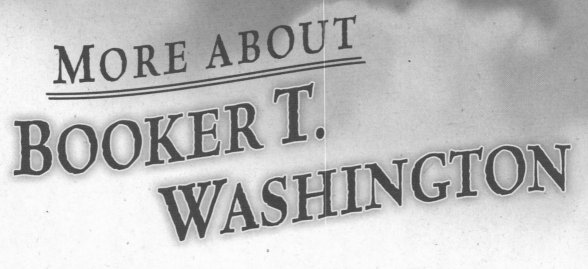

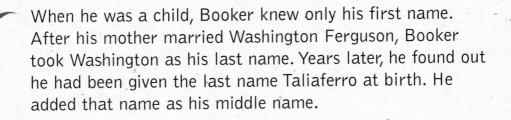

- Booker was born April 5, 1856, in Franklin County, Virginia. He was born into slavery, and his owner was James Burroughs.

- When he was a child, Booker knew only his first name. After his mother married Washington Ferguson, Booker took Washington as his last name. Years later, he found out he had been given the last name Taliaferro at birth. He added that name as his middle name.

- Theodore Roosevelt was sworn in as president on September 1, 1901. That same day, he sent a letter to Booker asking him to come to the White House. Booker was the first African American to dine at the White House.

- The man Booker hired to fight the grandfather clause in Alabama was a New York lawyer named Wilford H. Smith. To keep Booker's involvement in the case secret, Smith sent letters to Booker signed with a fake name.

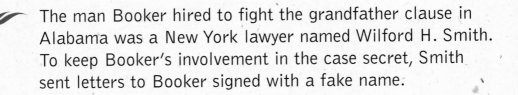

- Booker was part owner of the influential African American newspaper *New York Age*.

Booker was married three times during his life and had three children. He married Fannie Norton Smith in 1882, and she died in 1884. He married Olivia A. Davidson the next year, and she died in 1889. He married Margaret J. Murray in 1893. His daughter Portia Washington Pittman was from his marriage to Fannie. His sons, Booker Taliaferro Jr. and Ernest Davidson, were from his marriage to Olivia.

Booker's autobiography, *Up From Slavery*, was published in 1901. It became a bestseller and is still widely read.

Booker died November 14, 1915. He was buried on a hill overlooking Tuskegee Institute. Students made his brick tomb.

The Booker T. Washington National Monument was erected in Virginia on April 2, 1956.

GLOSSARY

Ku Klux Klan (KOO KLUHKS KLAN)—a group that promotes hate against African Americans, Catholics, Jews, immigrants, and other groups

plantation (plan-TAY-shuhn)—a large farm; before the Civil War, Southerners used slaves to work on their plantations.

Reconstruction (ree-kuhn-STRUHKT-shuhn)—the period of time following the Civil War when the U.S. government tried to rebuild Southern states

segregation (seg-ruh-GAY-shuhn)—the practice of keeping people or things apart from another group; some segregation laws prevented African Americans from using the same drinking fountains or theater entrances as whites.

INTERNET SITES

FactHound offers a safe, fun way to find Internet sites related to this book. All of the sites on FactHound have been researched by our staff.

Here's how:

1. Visit *www.facthound.com*
2. Type in this special code **0736846301** for age-appropriate sites. Or enter a search word related to this book for a more general search.
3. Click on the **Fetch It** button.

FactHound will fetch the best sites for you!

READ MORE

Collier, Christopher, and James Lincoln Collier. *Reconstruction and the Rise of Jim Crow, 1864–1896.* The Drama of American History. New York: Benchmark Books, 2000.

Frost, Helen. *Let's Meet Booker T. Washington.* Let's Meet Biographies. Philadelphia: Chelsea Clubhouse, 2004.

Isaacs, Sally Senzell. *Life on a Southern Plantation.* Picture the Past. Chicago: Heinemann Library, 2001.

Troy, Don. *W.E.B. Du Bois.* Journey to Freedom. Chanhassen, Minn.: Child's World, 1999.

BIBLIOGRAPHY

Ayers, Edward L. *The Promise of the New South: Life after Reconstruction.* New York: Oxford University Press, 1992.

Du Bois, Shirley Graham. *Booker T. Washington, Educator of Hand, Head, and Heart.* New York: Messner, 1955.

Harlan, Louis R. *Booker T. Washington: The Making of a Black Leader 1856–1901.* New York: Oxford University Press, 1975.

Thornbrough, Emma Lou, editor. *Booker T. Washington.* Great Lives Observed. Englewood Cliffs, N.J.: Prentice-Hall, 1969.

Washington, Booker T. *Up from Slavery: An Autobiography.* The Townsend Library. West Berlin, N.J.: Townsend Press, 2004.

INDEX